SUCCESS *is a* THIEF

SUCCESS *is a* THIEF

Inspirational Convocation Speeches

Edited by N. Ravichandran

PORTFOLIO PENGUIN

An imprint of Penguin Random House

PORTFOLIO

USA | Canada | UK | Ireland | Australia
New Zealand | India | South Africa | China | Singapore

Portfolio Books is part of the Penguin Random House group of companies whose addresses can be found at global.penguinrandomhouse.com

Published by Penguin Random House India Pvt. Ltd
4th Floor, Capital Tower 1, MG Road,
Gurugram 122 002, Haryana, India

Penguin Random House India

First Published by Random House India in 2015

10 9 8 7 6 5 4 3 2

ISBN 9788184007039

For sale in the Indian Subcontinent only

Typeset in Sabon by Manipal Digital Systems, Manipal
Printed at Repro India Limited

www.penguin.co.in

Contents

Editor's Note *vii*

Part A

1. Isher Judge Ahluwalia 3
2. Usha Ananthasubramanian 13
3. Subroto Bagchi 25
4. Ajay Banga 35
5. Arundhati Bhattacharya 47
6. Shekhar Dutt 57
7. R. Gopalakrishnan 69
8. A.P.J. Abdul Kalam 93
9. Roopa Kudva 113
10. Ranjana Kumar 125
11. Anand Mahindra 135
12. Arun Maira 147
13. R. Mukundan 161
14. Indra K. Nooyi 173
15. Deepak Parekh 187
16. Aroon Purie 207
17. S. Ramadorai 217

18. N. Ravichandran 235
19. Janmejaya Kumar Sinha 255
20. M.V. Subbiah 263

Part B

1. G. Narayana 275
2. Swami Nikhileshwarananda 283
3. N. Ravichandran 291
4. Madhusri Shrivastava 297

Part C

1. Debolina Dutta 309
2. Sundaravalli Narayanaswami 317
3. Balaraman Rajan 325

Acknowledgements 335

Editor's Note

Convocation is an important event in the educational journey of a student. It usually marks the end of an educational process and the beginning of an individual's professional journey. Often, convocation speeches (by eminent and accomplished individuals) survey the social, political, economic and cultural environment; identify potential and emerging wealth creation opportunities; motivate and inspire the graduating class to plan and realize a meaningful professional career in the context of their individual aspirations. Usually these addresses are inspirational, motivating and full of advice. These speeches are catalysts to rejuvenate and rekindle curiosity and creativity in an individual to meaningfully plan their personal and professional life.

The proposed compilation is designed in three parts. Part One, which is the core of this compilation, is a set of twenty-two convocation addresses delivered in various institutions of higher learning.

The second part of this compilation is a set of four articles on how to design inspirational speeches. The final part is a set of four invited reflections on the speeches from individuals from diverse backgrounds.

The primary motivation behind this volume is to bring inspirational/motivational speeches to young men and women in India who do not have the opportunity to study in some of the country's most reputed institutions, to enable them to read, experience and reflect on these addresses. It is expected that a deeper reflection will motivate them to realize their full potential in their professional and personal lives. Further, this compilation is motivated by the spirit advocated by Swami Vivekananda and my firm belief that such a rich collection of material should be made available to a wider audience to enhance public good.

This collection will help students, academicians and corporate trainers to learn and sharpen their skills in the area of (motivational) communication. In essence, it will provide an opportunity to learn how to conceive, write and deliver motivational and inspirational addresses.

This compilation is meant for undergraduate, graduate and PhD students as a complimentary academic material to their learning experience in their respective institutions. It will also serve as a reference book for teachers, academicians and practitioners in the industry to improve the effectiveness of their communication skills. It is aimed to be useful to professional motivational speakers and the academic fraternity specializing in inspirational communication.

Ahmedabad N. Ravichandran
23 April 2015

Part A

Isher Judge Ahluwalia

Dr Isher Judge Ahluwalia is a renowned Indian economist, with wide experience in the fields of economic growth, productivity, industrial and trade policy reforms, and urban planning and development. She is currently chairperson of the board of governors for the Indian Council for Research on International Economic Relations (ICRIER), a leading think tank based in New Delhi engaged in policy-oriented research. At ICRIER, Dr Ahluwalia is leading a major research and capacity-building programme on the challenges of urbanization in India. She was awarded the Padma Bhushan by the President of India in the year 2009 for her services in the field of education and literature.

Dr Ahluwalia was chairperson of the High Powered Expert Committee (HPEC) on Urban Infrastructure and Services during 2008–11; she was a member on the National Manufacturing Competitiveness Council and is on the boards of a number of premier research institutes in India. Dr Ahluwalia was vice chairperson of the Punjab State Planning Board from 2005 to 2007.

Dr Ahluwalia is on the board of trustees of International Water Management Institute (IWMI), and was chairperson, board of trustees of International Food Policy Research Institute (IFPRI), Washington DC, from 2003 to 2006. She was a member of the Eminent Persons Group (EPG) on India–ASEAN (Association of South East Asian Nations), an association established by the respective governments during the period 2011–12. She was also a member of the EPG of the Asian Development Bank from 2006 to 2007.

Dr Ahluwalia has written a number of books, the latest being *Transforming Our Cities: Postcards of Change*, and a co-edited volume titled *Urbanisation in India: Challenges, Opportunities and the Way Forward*, which proposes critical reforms and policy interventions. She also co-edited, together with Professor I.M.D. Little, *India's Economic Reforms and Development: Essays for Manmohan Singh.*

Isher Judge Ahluwalia

Dr Kiran Mazumdar-Shaw, chairperson, IIM Bangalore, Professor Devanath Tirupati, director, distinguished faculty and staff of IIM Bangalore, parents, family and friends of students and dear students, I feel honoured at being invited to deliver this address at the thirty-ninth annual convocation of IIM Bangalore, an institution of high learning and global standards. Let me begin by congratulating all of you, graduates, fellows, executives, policymakers and managers and leaders from the government and non-governmental sectors who have successfully completed your studies and have received your diplomas today, and especially those who have excelled with distinction and awards.

I am very impressed with the wide spectrum of courses covered at the institute and also your outreach to different stages in the careers of executives from the private sector, the public sector, the NGO sector and policymakers. The centres

---

Convocation address delivered by Ms Isher Judge Ahluwalia, Indian economist and chairperson, board of governors, the Indian Council for Research on International Economic Relations at the Indian Institute of Management Bangalore, on 27 March 2014. Reproduced with the permission of the author.

of excellence at IIM Bangalore have reached out to areas of growing importance such as corporate governance and social responsibility, software enterprise management, supply chain management, financial markets and risk management and also entrepreneurial learning. The centre for entrepreneurial learning, I understand, helps students to incubate their ideas and form start-ups, thus taking learning a step further. This is as it should be since IIM Bangalore is located in a city which has been the gateway to India's global competitiveness. Most recently, I was delighted to see that the ministry of urban development has chosen IIM Bangalore to nurture a centre of excellence in urban planning and management. Given the importance of urbanization in the current stage of our development, I cannot think of a better place than this to begin building our capacities in urban planning and management.

Half of India's population today is below the age of twenty-five. Most of you, graduating from the postgraduate programme in management (PGPM), belong to that half. This means that you, ladies and gentlemen, were literally cutting your teeth when India decided in 1991 to begin the process of opening up our economy to competition from foreign trade and investment. As you went to school and then college, you have seen India's economic growth accelerating from 5.5 per cent per annum in the 1990s to close to 8 per cent per annum in the following decade. It is only reasonable to expect that you will not settle for anything less.

My own view is that the recent major slowdown in growth is an aberration and can be corrected through appropriate policies. I also believe that once the irreducible uncertainty associated with an election is over, no matter which government comes to power, growth will pick up.

The period from 2001 to 2011 was a period of rapid growth of the kind India had never seen before. This growth was driven by the private sector and led by the services sector. If IT, BPO, financial services and healthcare services played a major role in this acceleration, then the pharmaceuticals, auto-components and automotive sectors displayed the global competitiveness of some of our manufacturing sectors. The percentage of population in poverty declined to 25 per cent, although there were legitimate demands for raising the poverty threshold. The long-standing issues of health, education, inclusion and poverty alleviation were beginning to be addressed, though not adequately.

Faster growth itself was not without its stresses. First and foremost, the growth of employment did not keep pace with the growth of output in the non-agricultural sectors, and there were periods when employment in the formal sector even declined. Expanding employment opportunities in the industry and services sectors, which provide scope for high-productivity jobs, continue to be the principal challenge for policymakers as we aim for faster, more inclusive and sustainable economic growth in the years to come. It is the only sustainable instrument to make our growth inclusive. The decade of 2001–11 had to grapple with the old challenges of inadequate and poor quality infrastructure and macroeconomic vulnerability, while it also faced the new challenges of skill deficits and unplanned urbanization.

I propose to speak on the challenges of urbanization in India. Before I do that, let me say that if we are to experience sustained growth rates of 7 to 8 per cent per annum, faster growth of GDP has to come from industry and services, since agriculture at best can grow at 4 to 4.5 per cent per annum. The urban share of GDP is currently estimated at about 63 per cent (of GDP) and this is projected to increase to 75 per cent by 2030–31. This implies that urbanization will gather momentum in the years to come.

As of 2011, we had only 31 per cent of our population living in urban areas, compared with 48 per cent in China, 83 per cent in Korea and 87 per cent in Brazil. India's urban population is projected to increase to 40 per cent by 2030–31, which I believe is an underestimate. As the Indian economy resumes its journey to 7 to 8 per cent growth, many cities will experience peripheral expansion, with smaller municipalities and large villages surrounding the core city becoming part of the metropolitan area. We will also need more cities acting as engines of growth for providing the economies of agglomeration.

We economists have often identified the investment climate with ease of doing business. Actually, the investment climate is as much about the ease of living as about the ease of doing business. Even if we were to reduce the transactions cost of doing business to zero, who would want to invest in our industry and services sectors if our cities cannot provide the basic amenities of everyday living and civic infrastructure for public health, for example, clean water and sanitation? If we are to attract skilled persons like you, people who will bring in innovations, create employment opportunities, generate wealth and help raise the standards of living of our people, then we need to improve significantly the state of our cities so that our cities can compete with alternative destinations abroad which are waiting with open arms for people like you. In fact, we need to use your management training to fix the state of our cities.

Our cities are visibly deficient in the services they provide. You are all familiar with the challenges of getting from one place to another in Bengaluru and the constant pressure of congestion and pollution. Be it solid waste management or waste water treatment or availability of drinking water from a treated source; or public transport and the state of our roads, pavements and traffic support infrastructure; or, indeed, the conservation of green spaces, the state of our cities is far from what we should expect for basic living comfort. It is also far short of what is needed to realize their economic potential.

But I bring some good news to you. Change in urban India is not only in the air, but is beginning to show on the ground. I have travelled extensively over the last five years to Indian cities and towns—large and small—and I find that some cities have brought about a transformation we would not have thought possible in a short period of time. Whether it is continuous water supply from a treated source for all in the small town of Malkapur in Maharashtra, or inspiring stories of solid waste management in Pune, Rajkot and Pammal, or waste water treatment in Navi Mumbai, Surat and Chandigarh, or improvement in the public transport scenario through buses in Bengaluru and the BRTS in Ahmedabad, Indian cities are on the road to transforming themselves. Similarly, e-governance with back-end integration has made a significant difference to our travails of getting birth or death certificates, or building sanctions, or paying property tax and/or utility bills. Bengaluru in Karnataka, Hyderabad in Andhra Pradesh, Kalyan Dombivili, Pune and Pimpri Chinchwad in Maharashtra, and Ahmedabad and Surat in Gujarat are only some of these cities.

In all these cases, the capacity to plan and manage at the local level, an enabling environment provided by the state government, human leadership and the use of new technology, particularly IT, has played a major role in bringing about the transformation. A major game changer has been a strategic initiative by the Government of India to launch the Jawaharlal Nehru National Urban Renewal Mission (JNNURM) in 2005 in partnership with the state governments, which has not only provided a large part of the funds but also nudged the state governments and city governments to carry out certain reforms.

While I have been documenting this transformation in my recent writings, we need to look deeper into what has made this possible and put the capacities, institutions and policies in place across the urban landscape of India. I realize that as you, PGPM graduates, step into the real world looking for opportunities of employment and enterprise, the world will be your playfield. Some of you will join multinational corporations with offices in different parts of the world. Others may find opportunities in India in the private sector or in the government or non-governmental sectors. I hope that the crying need for better management of our cities will also attract your attention as you make this transition from learning to the marketplace.

Wherever you are, you will be striving to give your best. IIM Bangalore has shown you the way by benchmarking itself against global best standards and practices. I wish you well in your chosen assignments. For those of you who have taken time out from your busy careers to learn and reflect, you will go back to your assignments with renewed vigour. The challenges before our economy and our society are formidable, particularly since we have chosen the democratic way. I am confident that, with your training in this institution of excellence, you will help shape contemporary India through model governance practices and shared social responsibility. Congratulations once again, and thank you for giving me this opportunity to share my thoughts.

Usha Ananthasubramanian

Smt. Usha Ananthasubramanian is the chairman and managing director of Bharatiya Mahila Bank Ltd, the first of its kind in the Indian banking industry.

She holds a master's degree in statistics from the University of Madras and a master's degree in ancient Indian culture from the University of Mumbai.

In a career spanning over three decades, she has worked in various positions in the banking and allied areas. She started her career with the Life Insurance Corporation of India (LIC). She joined the banking industry in February 1982 as a specialist officer in the planning stream of the Bank of Baroda and rose to the rank of general manager and has held many key positions in the bank. She was closely associated with the transformation project of the Bank of Baroda, including rebranding and innovative HR initiatives.

Prior to taking over as chairman and managing director of the bank, she was the executive director of the Punjab National Bank (PNB) for over two years. When at PNB, she was part of the committee formed for examination of the blue print and other related tasks for setting up of the first women-focused bank of India. She was the head of the core management team constituted by the ministry of finance, Government of India, for coordinating the process of establishment of the bank.

Under her leadership, the bank has launched several innovative, women-friendly products—both assets and liability products and also technology-enabled products and services.

Her hobbies include reading English, Tamil and Sanskrit literature, music, and she has a flair for learning languages. She is also a trained Carnatic musician and plays the veena.

She is a regular speaker at national and international conferences and seminars on various themes including banking, women empowerment, governance, education and gender issues. She regularly contributes for journals and magazines.

She is a member of the national think tank for the poorest states and the inclusive growth programme of the department for international development and also chairs the FICCI committee on financial inclusion.

Usha Ananthasubramanian

Respected Shri. J.J. Irani, chairman of the board of governors of the Indian Institute of Management Lucknow, members of the board of governors, Professor Rajiv Srivastava, director, IIM Lucknow, faculty members, family and friends of the graduating students, graduating students, good evening! I stand here with great respect for the tremendous human potential before me. If I am here before you, I have to thank my parents, teachers, mentors and well-wishers who have helped me remove the stones and thorns from my path, and have held my hand to lead me in the right direction.

It is indeed a special privilege and an honour for me to be here with you today as part of the twenty-ninth convocation of the institute, and to deliver the convocation address. I thank the organizers for giving me this opportunity to be part of this important occasion. The atmosphere is highly inspiring, intense, emotional, and yet peaceful, pleasant and extremely calm.

Convocation address delivered by Smt. Usha Ananthasubramanian, chairman and managing director of Bharatiya Mahila Bank Ltd, at the Indian Institute of Management Lucknow on 14 March 2015. Reproduced with the permission of the author.

At the outset, I convey my heartiest congratulations to all the students who have received their diplomas and medals. I wish you the best of the best in your journey forward and I am sure you will make a substantial difference, not only to yourself, your family and your community, but also to the country and the world at large. I also congratulate the faculty whose dedication and involvement have gone into creating such a brand of students. This is a notable achievement. I also congratulate the parents, friends and well-wishers who have nurtured dreams for you and have supported you in your journey to this destination of achievement.

You are all seeds sown in fire. It is normal that a seed sown in the soil, provided with the right amount of water, sunlight and manure—and protected from the cattle with a fence—germinates and grows. It is only a surprise if this does not happen. But the acorns, the seeds of oak trees, are said to be so hard that they burst only in a forest fire, and with the torrential rain that follows, they sprout and grow into strong trees that live for hundreds of years. Having gone through the rigours of an IIM education you are a confident lot today . . . a toughened lot today . . . a robust lot today.

My dear young friends, today is an important day in your lives and this day marks a significant milestone in your life's journey. IIM Lucknow is the fourth of its kind in the country and it is indeed prestigious for each one of you to be a student of this campus. You entered into the institution after facing intense competition and earning your diploma by your hard work, and you have embarked upon the academic trip with great dedication. This is a proud moment for you, your teachers, parents—all those who had any part in shaping your life thus far. Though your mission for higher learning began here, you know for sure that it does not end here. Learning is a continuous process. It does not end till you feel fully confident with regard to meeting the challenges and uncertainties of life, and dealing with the successes and failures with a positive attitude. Life is full of challenges and uncertainties and so you will always be driving with the 'L' board.

The greatest strength and wealth of any nation is its youth population. In the hands of its youth rests the future of a nation. And the quality of its youth determines the kind of future the nation will have. The youth makes up about 35 per cent of the total population of our country, and this 35 per cent constitutes the country's future. This powerhouse of the nation needs to be harnessed to reach newer heights. The creative potential of the younger generation, coupled with their zeal, enthusiasm, energy and versatility, can bring about phenomenal transformation in the country. It is, therefore, important to empower our youth, who are a storehouse of infinite energy, and who will lead us into a better tomorrow.

Today, you are equipped with a diploma from an institute of high repute and are entering into the world to experiment and experience newer vistas of life. Being digital natives, you are guided by technology in all your endeavours. You are all products of the demographic divide; we all look to you to create a nation with high global standards and benchmarks—a nation that will emerge as an economic superpower. You will be the torch bearers of the nation that has started soaring forward. The ambitious programmes, 'Make in India' and 'Skill India' are in the hands of talented youths like you.

I am sure each one of you has a bundle of dreams and aspirations to give shape to. By making them a reality, you will achieve newer heights in life.

As I was completing my postgraduation, one of my professors at the university told me his wish for me: I should encounter grand and magnificent failures. I was baffled to hear this and he was quick to react to my confused expression. He told me failures are beautiful, interesting and inspiring, and lessons learnt last throughout life. Success can be intoxicating, exciting, thrilling and sensational, and can also pull you down. Success cannot teach great lessons, as failures do. Failure also has the capacity to teach you to fight to the last and never give up. It teaches you the satisfaction of having given your best and the attitude to better the best next time. There is a difference between a rival and an enemy. It is healthy for us to have rivals; we must pray that we are blessed with great rivals, who help us better our best every time.

Two key drivers of success in life are passion and determination, which undergo many moments of testing. Such moments are the times when you need to face obstacles. The deciding factor is how steadfast and passionate you are with regard to your dreams, and how diligently you work to overcome obstacles. The best lessons in life are not learnt from books or libraries but by studying fellow human beings around us. The more you observe, the more you learn. Even the world's best business plan will not produce any returns if it is not backed by passion and integrity. More than theoretical views and bookishness, I would like to be more into proven, real-life stories and happenings, and share a few of them. One such story is that of the Brooklyn Bridge, which many of us see, admire and take pride in having crossed.

In *Pour Your Heart Into It*, Howard Scultz, chairman and CEO of Starbucks Coffee Company, says, 'Life is a series of near misses. But a lot of what we ascribe to luck is not luck at all. It's seizing the day and accepting responsibility for your future. It's seeing what other people don't see, and pursing that vision, no matter who tells you not to.'

Engineer John Roebling decided that he would build the world's longest bridge to connect Long Island with New York, and would build it in a new way. But his way was too new. The idea was shot down by experts, who called it an impossible feat as there was no other bridge of its size at that time. There was tremendous opposition to his idea and he was persuaded to drop his plan. It took fifteen years to convince people that it would work. His dream was driven by passion, which kept telling him that his conception of the bridge was right. His only source of support was his upcoming engineer son, Washington Roebling. The father-son team prepared a detailed plan and got the required team on board. Though the bottlenecks were well thought out and mitigation was in place, a tragic accident at the site occurred a few months after the building started, killing the senior Roebling.

Given this loss, it was normal for anyone to give up but the junior Roebling was determined to make his father's vision come true. It was yet another setback when Washington suffered brain damage and was injured to the extent of being absolutely immobile with the exception of one finger. The experts who had claimed that building the bridge was impossible called both the Roeblings crazy fools. In view of

Washington's inability to extend his services, there was a call to scrap the project. But Washington stood determined and passionate, being very clear about his objective. He depended entirely on his wife, Emily Roebling, to communicate through the only movable part of his body—the single finger. He developed a code to make her understand his communication. Again, his idea received a lot of criticism. Instructions were interpreted by his wife and relayed to the engineers and, thirteen years later, the Brooklyn Bridge was complete. This spectacular landmark, made operational on 24 May 1883, was the longest suspension bridge in the world at the time.

There are a number of lessons that may be gleaned from this true story, but the most important message is that of passion and determination, and the idea that we must never give up.

Passion for excellence is an unending journey and the presence of this quality makes every act beautiful. Passion for excellence is everywhere—from the way you throw waste paper into the bin to the way you complete a project. Here again, I am reminded of a little story. A king once visited a temple under construction, where he saw a sculptor making an idol. Suddenly, he noticed a similar idol lying nearby. Surprised, he asked the sculptor, 'Do you need two statues of the same idol?' 'No,' said the sculptor without looking up. 'We need only one, but the first one got damaged at the last stage.' The king examined the idol and found no apparent damage. 'Where is the damage?' he asked. 'There is a scratch on the nose of the idol,' said the sculptor, still busy with his work. 'Where are you going to install the idol?' asked the king. The sculptor replied that it would be installed on a pillar 30 feet high. 'If the idol is that far away, who is going to know that there is a scratch on the nose?' the king asked. The sculptor stopped his work, looked up at the king, smiled and said, 'I will know it.' The desire to excel does not depend upon whether someone else appreciates it or not. Excellence is a drive from inside, not outside. Excellence is not for someone else to notice but for your own satisfaction. Passion for excellence is more important than having passion alone.

Self-accomplishment and direction of intelligence are twin keys for success in life.

Certainly, the story of Roger Bannister, who overcame barriers by suitably directing his intelligence, is an amazing testimonial to the power of one's personal belief. For hundreds of years experts believed that no man could break the four-minute mile, and this was true. Whoever attempted this suffered serious cardiac problems. However, one person with an incredibly powerful belief in himself had another idea. He was quoted saying, 'I believe this is not a dream. It is my reality.' And indeed it was, for on that blustery day, 6 May 1954, Roger Bannister beat the unthinkable four-minute-mile barrier and perhaps, in a sense, did away with mankind's perceived limits to self-accomplishment; Roger Bannister had accomplished more than his reality. He had proven the unlimited possibilities of mankind! How could he do it? In order to run a mile in less than four minutes, people were training their legs, calves, knees and toes, not realizing the actual impediment was the heart. While everyone focused on the legs in order to run a mile in less than four minutes, Roger Bannister focused on the heart, which had to be empowered to pump that kind of blood. In the next one year, 304 people ran a mile in less than four minutes! He had defined the problem clearly, believed in self-accomplishment, rightly applied his intelligence and worked to achieve the impossible.

Passion and passion for excellence, personal belief and direction of intelligence lead to the joy of creating something new and making it a success. The new bank we have created, Bharatiya Mahila Bank Ltd, is conceptually new, being a segment-specific bank. Setting up a bank entails a host of activities and the reckoning starts only from the day the regulator grants the licence. In the case of our bank, the time between the dates of licensing and the launching of the bank was just fifty-five days. Many challenges had to be overcome to see the bank emerge on the appointed day with full technology, people, products, systems, procedures and readiness to operate. Nothing like this has been created in banking history and the pressure to perform made us look at certain innovative options like drawing people from the existing public sector banks and incentivizing them with a higher grade placement, outsourced technology from a cost, time and people point of view, and at the same time ensuring data security, timeliness and product innovations. We had been through a crucible of tests of various kinds but creating, shaping and heading a new organization has given me immense joy. Organizations are usually uni-cultural, but with people from more than twenty banks walking into a new set-up, the Bharatiya Mahila Bank has the uniqueness of a multicultural organization. Every new creation fraught with challenges is also a pack of excitement.

You have multiple choices when it comes to which career to embrace but choose the one where you derive greater satisfaction and are always able to better the best. You are among the few fortunate persons who have had access to educational experience at this well-known institution and I am sure this experience will be rewarding to you all through your life. You are already part of the realities of intense competition and you have been made capable of taking advantage of the highly competitive environment. Your training and qualifications can help you create wealth and welfare for you, your family and the organizations you work for. There is also a small duty awaiting you—to endeavour for the well-being of the society. The values of caring and sharing, service and sacrifice have kept our society vibrant and beautiful, making the earth a lovely planet to live on. As citizens of this nation, we have inherited noble values and a concern for fellow human beings. You should aspire to deepen and widen your knowledge horizons, experience the power of teamwork and be guided by higher values in which you have conviction.

Let me conclude with a famous poem from Rabindranath Tagore's *Gitanjali.*

Where the mind is without fear and the head is held high
Where knowledge is free
Where the world has not been broken up into fragments by narrow domestic walls
Where words come out from the depth of truth
Where tireless striving stretches its arms towards perfection
Where the clear stream of reason has not lost its way into the dreary desert sand of dead habit

Where the mind is led forward by thee into ever-widening thought and action
Into that heaven of freedom, my Father, let my country awake.

Once again, I convey my heartiest congratulations to all of you who have received diplomas today and also to the teachers, family, friends and well-wishers who have nurtured a dream for you and groomed and guided you to face the world and its challenges, and emerge as achievers.

I wish each one of you all the very best in all your efforts and endeavours!

Subroto Bagchi

A leading IT industry innovator, Subroto Bagchi co-founded Mindtree in 1999 with a vision to engineer meaningful technology solutions that help businesses and societies flourish. Under his leadership, Mindtree has grown from a technology start-up to a $580+ million enterprise with more than 14,000 Mindtree Minds in twenty-five offices around the globe. Prior to being named the Mindtree chairman in 2012, Bagchi held various leadership roles including as the chief operating officer, for the first eight years of Mindtree's journey.

Bagchi's leadership development, marketing and knowledge management initiatives have differentiated the company from competitors since Mindtree's inception. Today, Mindtree helps 1000 global companies solve their greatest technology challenges by combining the expertise of a large firm, the agility of a smaller company, and a high-touch, collaborative culture. This innovative approach has led to several industry awards, such as the 'Best Managed IT/Software/Technology Company in Asia' and the 'Best Managed Company in India' for 2013 by Euromoney. Mindtree has also been named, 'Most Promising Company of 2013' by CNBC and recognized as one of the top-four companies globally in talent development for 2014 in the Association for Talent Development (ATD)'s BEST award.

Throughout his career, Bagchi has been highly acclaimed for his visionary leadership. A thirty-five-year veteran of the computer industry, Bagchi was chief executive of Wipro's global research and development, and set up Wipro's US operations, converting research and development (R&D) from being a cost centre to a profit centre. Following Wipro, he moved to Lucent Technologies where he started their Bell Development Center in Bangalore, India.

Bagchi is also the chairman of White Swan Foundation, a not-for-profit organization that offers knowledge services in the area of mental health.

In addition to being chairman of Mindtree, Bagchi is India's bestselling business author, with four published business books, including *The High Performance Entrepreneur*. Bagchi is also an active supporter of social causes like mental health, blindness, geriatric care and engineering innovation through his work with the White Swan Foundation, Aravind Eye Hospital, Nightingales Trust–Bagchi Center for Active Ageing, and the School of Engineering, University of Florida. He studied political science at Utkal University, India.

Subroto Bagchi

Dean Cammy Abernathy, esteemed members of faculty and staff, family and friends congregated to witness today's graduation ceremony and, most importantly, my dear graduating students.

I cannot tell you how honoured I feel to be in your midst today. I feel deeply grateful that you have bestowed the honour on me and, through me, on Mindtree, the enterprise I co-founded fifteen years ago. As we built what is now an IT services company with 13,000 people, we chose to set up our US Development Center here at Gainesville. This centre is a three-way collaboration between your university, the state of Florida, and Mindtree. We chose to come here largely because of the reputation of the University of Florida.

Given our relationship, when Dean Abernathy asked me to be your commencement speaker, I was delighted. But then I asked her: do students really listen to commencement speeches, particularly from people two or three times their age? Dean Abernathy replied emphatically, 'Yes, young

---

Convocation address delivered by Mr Subroto Bagchi, co-founder, Mindtree at the University of Florida, Gainsville, Florida, on 3 May 2014. Reproduced with the permission of the author.

people listen, they pay attention. In particular, they want to be inspired.' Then she said something I will never forget. She said, 'Our job is to inspire young people. You cannot inspire them enough.'

Drowned in the ordinariness of our existence, sometimes dealing with our own struggles and frustrations, and during the occasional, inevitable moments of cynicism, we adults often forget the responsibility to inspire. But we can never inspire enough. We cannot just say that we did our bit and that no more needs to be done.

To my graduating student friends, I give you the words of your dean: your job and mine will always be to inspire. And we can never inspire enough!

You have already begun.

I asked you to write to me with your questions and with your thoughts on what you wanted to hear from me at Commencement today. As your responses poured in, I marvelled at the quality of your intellect and the power of your humanity. You sent in questions that astonished me with their thoughtfulness, kindness and wisdom. You revealed your ambitions, your fears, your strength and your fragility. You took my breath away.

One question in particular moved me deeply, touching on matters of change and identity, on how to keep one's sense of self in an ever-changing environment. Your classmate Elise Burke wrote, and I paraphrase only slightly:

As a student about to enter a new world, I have this feeling of loss. I'm sure it is something that we all must be feeling: that, by graduating, we are potentially losing a part of ourselves. How does one deal with that, morph that into a new world, and ease the weird, empty feeling that comes with graduating and entering the unknown? How do we keep ourselves?

You are not alone. Everyone seated here has felt this way at some point. These have been my feelings when I left college, and then when I left my professional life to start a company at twenty-eight; I felt that way again when that company folded up and I began working as a manager in a large corporation, and then when I left that contented but cocooned life to co-found Mindtree fifteen years ago. Even now as I stand here in front of you, that 'weird, empty feeling' is coming back to me as I contemplate the inevitable transition that will happen for me in a few years from now.

That you are potentially losing a part of yourself will be a recurring theme for the rest of your life and you will find yourself asking, 'How do I morph into a new world, ease the weird, empty feeling that comes from entering the unknown, and keep my sense of self?'

One day, a few years from now, perhaps you will find yourself sitting in your tiny home-office, pensive because you had to sell your start-up company, which was your baby, because if you hadn't, it would have shut down. And you will be asking yourself these very same questions.

You will ask them when you are sitting in your office in the White House, alone except for the sound of a janitor's vacuum cleaner out in the hallway. You will have just completed your second term in office and tomorrow, after eight years, you will no longer be the President of the country.

The questions will come to you when you leave your comfortable, glamorous job as the CEO of a Fortune 100 firm, because you have decided to take on the responsibility of turning around a struggling international relief organization.

And you know what? The questions will rise again as you move in and out of some very precious relationships in your personal life.

So, Elise, you have put your finger on a vein that pulses below the cheers and celebrations of the day: the idea of change. How will you handle it? How will you make the trade-offs? How will you deal with the loss? How will you survive this?

You will; I'll say that first. You will do all this, and more, and you will do it with courage, humility and grace. But before I say any more, I'd like you to pause and picture yourself right now. What do you see? Graduation robes, a big smile, a funny hat with a tassel on it? Look again, at the images layered below. Go all the way back to your first day at university. There you are: excited, uncertain, happy, sad, mixed-up, with your two suitcases, your six overflowing cardboard boxes of random but precious things, in the unadorned dorm room that will be home now.

From that day, to this day: look at what you have done. You have been the master of change. From our vantage point today, that change might appear to be a smooth curve, but it wasn't. There were bumps. There were high highs and low lows. You took it all in stride, and here you are. The change that you have navigated in these four years is really no different from the change you will navigate when you start a family, or leave a plush job for a meaningful one, or when, one day, you drop your own child off on the first day of kindergarten and try not to cry as he or she vanishes from sight.

You see, you are not graduating with simply an engineering degree. You are graduating with a rope, a pickaxe, hooks, a water bottle and a walkie-talkie to help you navigate all the curves ahead. Yesterday you were good.

Tomorrow you will be superb. But today you do not know it yet. This is humility. This is the beginning of wisdom.

Consider the river. At its source, nothing about it suggests greatness or grandeur. The Amazon, when you trace it all the way back to the Apacheta cliff in Arequipa, Peru, begins as a glacial stream. Nearby are just a few lumps of snow below a solitary wooden cross that seems to say, simply, keep the faith. At her source high up in the Himalayas, the Ganges is just a tiny gush. It is the same story for many great rivers in the world.

At her source, the river has no control over what is ahead; all she can do is flow on to just the one next step. And the next. And then one more. At that time, actually, she isn't even a river. She is just a stream, a rivulet. But as she gurgles along, she finds another one to join her. The rivulet welcomes the tributary. Now they become a river.

As this river now flows with new energy, there appears a huge mountain, blocking her path. The river doesn't fight the mountain, and neither does she flow back to where she came from. The river finds her patient way around the mountain. The journey becomes beautiful once more.

Then suddenly, out of nothing, nowhere, the surface below and the banks by the side vanish. What appears is a monstrous gorge below. What happens now? The river does not weep. The river becomes a roaring waterfall.

Every waterfall in the world roars even as it falls! And guess what? The sun illuminates its mist, and a rainbow appears, and the entire world comes to marvel at its majesty.

Through the trickle, the tributary and the torrent, an expansive, deep calm emerges. The river's benevolent flow creates life; civilizations flourish along its banks; and then it becomes one with the ocean. But at the source, the river has no idea of what it will become, or where it will go.

If the river were to speak to you today, what would she say?

The river would say: Your identity is evolving; it is okay to have self-doubt. Uncertainty is inherent in change, and change is the only thing that is certain.

The river would say: Don't just be passionate—do something. Passion is what passion does. Changing the world happens with one tiny step at a time. If you are an idea-person, if you dream big, if you are ambitious and creative, then you probably want to build something big and make a big impact. But you probably also know the feeling of being overwhelmed by the enormity of what you need to do and what you hope to accomplish. But like the Amazon at its source, just take that one next step.

As you flow on, from source to confluence to estuary, sometimes even your very best will not be enough.

Sometimes you will falter. Sometimes you will make poor decisions with unpleasant outcomes. The river would say: Every single day, you get the chance to start all over again. The river would say: Don't dwell on failing; instead, prepare to succeed. And when you fall, fall like me! Fall brilliantly.

Along the path, there will be loss. The river would say: Honour your feelings of loss, but do not wallow in them.

Loss is not the boss of you. To flow, we must leave something behind. Each step we take is always a step further.

Change comes sometimes from the outside world and sometimes from within. Sometimes we see it coming, and sometimes it catches us off guard. Sometimes we are able to bend with it and withstand it. Sometimes it knocks us over and leaves us breathless. And sometimes we ride it to glorious new tomorrows.

Today, each one of you leaves behind certain markers of who you are: volleyball player, honours student, champion French fries eater, debater, essay writer, student leader. But you carry with you the seeds of all the things that you are. And you will find new markers that point to those things that you are: entrepreneur, engineer, activist, change maker, parent, business leader. Whatever may be your goal, flow with abandon and intensity; make friends with passers-by; welcome every tributary; and, when the gorge opens its jaws, fall and find new force.

Be like the Amazon. Even the mighty ocean will wait with respect for your arrival.

I urge you to embrace a life of not just courage but wisdom, not just capability but credence, not just glory but greatness. Rejoice in your arrival this evening. May your tomorrows be enchanted. As you chart your new life, may you inherit the greatness of your parents, your teachers and your friends. As your legacy, may humanity be richer, wiser and more inspired because of you. And remember: you can never inspire enough.

Thank you for sharing today's wonderful occasion with me. My wife Susmita and our daughters, Neha and Niti, are here with me this evening, applauding your achievements and wishing you the very best in your continuing journey.

I am grateful to the many people who helped me in the process of creating this speech: the team at the University of Florida, including Dean Cammy Abernathy, Dr Angela Lindner, Teresa Cocherell and Heather Ashley; the team at Mindtree, including Shilpa Kona, Samantha Rist and Nandini S.H.; and the graduating students who sent in their questions. And finally, to my daughter, Neha Bagchi, for her help in sense-making and editing: thank you.

Ajay Banga

Ajay Banga is president and chief executive officer of MasterCard and a member of its board of directors.

Prior to joining MasterCard in 2009, Mr Banga was chief executive officer of Citigroup Asia Pacific, responsible for all businesses in the region, including institutional banking, alternative investments, wealth management, consumer banking and credit cards. He joined Citigroup in 1996 and held a variety of senior management roles in the United States, Asia Pacific, Europe, Middle East and Africa. He was also responsible for Citi's brand marketing and from 2005 to 2009 oversaw its efforts in microfinance.

Mr Banga began his career at Nestlé, India, where for thirteen years he worked on assignments spanning sales, marketing and general management. He also spent two years at PepsiCo, where he was instrumental in launching its fast-food franchises in India as the economy liberalized.

Mr Banga is a member of the board of overseers of the Weill Cornell Medical College and a member of the board of governors of the American Red Cross. Mr Banga is a member of President Obama's Advisory Committee for Trade Policy and Negotiations. He serves on the US–India CEO Forum and is chairman of the US–India Business Council.

Mr Banga is also a member of each of the following: the executive committee of the Business Roundtable, the international business council of the World Economic Forum, the Council on Foreign Relations, the Economic Club of New York and the Business Council, on which he is a vice chair.

Mr Banga serves on the board of directors of the following organizations: the Financial Services Roundtable—where he is chairman-elect, the New York City Ballet and the Partnership for New York City. He also serves on the International Advisory Board of the Moscow School of Management (SKOLKOVO). He is a fellow of the Foreign Policy Association and was awarded the Foreign Policy Association Medal in 2012.

From 2007 to 2012, Mr Banga served on the board of directors of Kraft Foods. He has also served on the board of trustees of the Asia Society, the New York Hall of Science and the National Urban League, among others.

He received a BA in Economics from Delhi University where he graduated with honours and is an alumnus of the Indian Institute of Management Ahmedabad.

Ajay Banga

Congratulations!

Chairman Naik and members of the board of governors, Director Nanda, faculty, families and, above all, to the graduating class of 2015, congratulations! Well done! You came to IIM Ahmedabad to forge your own destiny, to shape your own future. You understood what Tagore wrote so many years ago: 'You can't cross the sea merely by standing and staring at the water'.

Tonight, we can say that the waters that first beckoned you here have now been crossed, and that you have reached a farther shore. What a great moment! To those who have supported, loved and nurtured you along the way—families, faculty and friends—this achievement is yours as well.

It means a great deal to me to be back here thirty-four years after my own convocation. To join all of you in recognizing this year's outstanding graduates, to gather here at Louis Kahn

---

Convocation address delivered by Mr Ajay Banga, president and chief executive officer of MasterCard, at the Indian Institute of Management Ahmedabad, on 21 March 2015. Reproduced with the permission of the author.

Plaza—which is as stunning and grand as ever—and to mark the fiftieth anniversary of IIM Ahmedabad's first convocation.

This is truly a privilege of a lifetime.

IIM Ahmedabad's fiftieth convocation

When you look back fifty years, you find some interesting milestones. For example, fifty years ago, IBM introduced the computer mainframe; the first Star Trek pilot was made; and Warren Buffett became the head of Berkshire Hathaway. By the way, a $100 investment in Berkshire in 1965 would be worth nearly $2 million today. There is of course an even greater investment that's been made since then: the investment in the education of leaders here in India and around the world, thanks to this institution. It's an investment that we pay tribute to tonight and continue to be grateful for a half century later.

Homecoming

Coming back here invokes a wellspring of wonderful memories. It's a homecoming of sorts. This school gave me a great education. It gave me a family. I met my wife here, who is in the audience tonight. That meeting produced a lifelong partnership that is the bedrock of my joy and happiness. It also gave us the most precious gifts of all—our two daughters. So, not only does IIM Ahmedabad rank among the world's elite business schools, it also possesses the alchemy for matchmaking! In a broader sense, IIM Ahmedabad has also given my wife—Ritu—and me an extended family of very dear friends and a robust network of contacts.

A number of these friends are in the audience this evening: Chintan Parikh—a member of your board, and Vinayak Chatterjee—chairman of Feedback Infrastructure and probably one of my closest friends, who flew in for this evening with his wife. Today, I wish for each of you equal richness in gifts I've received from this school.

Class of 2015— Celebrating their journey

To the class of 2015, I want to begin by celebrating the journey you guys have been on. I couldn't be more delighted and thrilled for you! It feels just like yesterday when I was in your shoes . . . sitting where you are sitting. Granted, yesterday was more like three and a half decades ago. But that's the kind of impression this school makes on you. You never really leave it and it never really leaves you. I remember some seriously hard courses, brilliant but demanding professors, more than a few late nights and the first year—realizing that if you can survive that, you can survive anything. I remember having the experience of a lifetime—forming friendships and bonds that would last a lifetime. I wish all of that and more for all of you as well.

Thanks to Director Nanda, I got a chance to meet with some of this year's class when I was here this January for Vibrant Gujarat. I had spent the better part of that week working with today's leaders in business, government, international development and other fields. Then I came here to the campus, where I got to spend time with tomorrow's leaders in those fields. Needless to say, it was a beautiful symmetry.

So, what I want to focus on in my talk this evening is leadership. *Your* leadership. How do you take the leadership potential you have and cultivate it so that you can begin to realize it along your journey? None of this is to say I have all the answers. I don't. My daughters who are about your age will tell you that. What I do have are some perspectives on leadership that I can offer. I'll share three:

First, I'll share some leadership attributes that I look for in myself and others.

Second, I'll talk about leadership and the importance of developing a global view of things.

Third, I'll talk about why leadership in its highest form facilitates doing well and doing good.

But before I proceed, I want to offer the following disclaimer: when I graduated, I was all of twenty-one—wet behind the ears. And I had no clue what I was going to do with my life, other than join a great global firm like Nestlé. That was my grand plan: Get with somebody good; get with somebody global; do something that interested me—that's it. So, don't stress if you haven't got a detailed plan for your life. Anyone can have a good idea or plan; what makes it great is execution, which brings me to my first point around leadership attributes.

1. Leadership attributes

In sharing these leadership attributes with you, I'm going to repeat some points I have made over the past year to other business schools. The first is a sense of urgency. Today's world of rapidly advancing technology and ever-shortening innovation cycles has no space for procrastination. It's that urgency that makes me say to colleagues in my company, 'If you have good news for me, take the stairs. If you have bad news, take the elevator.' I need that information fast, so I can do something about it.

The second is a sense of balance. A lot of people think that urgency and patience are contradictory. And they could not be more wrong. You need to be patient enough to listen to everybody, but yet, you must have a sense of urgency to take a decision and to execute it.

The third is to be courageous enough to take thoughtful risks. Rarely are you going to have perfect information. The willingness to take a decision at that time will depend on your ability to take a thoughtful risk, which ultimately depends on your courage. The thoughtful part depends also on your humility and realizing that you don't have all the answers—that you can learn something from everybody. You get a good dose of humility as you soon as you arrive here. You come from a school where you were the top gun. You get here and everybody's a top gun.

And the fourth is to be paranoid—competitively paranoid. And by that I don't mean be fearful. What I mean is, constantly ask yourself if you are missing something. Is there more to the problem? If you don't question everything, if you're not competitively paranoid, you will not have the sense of introspection that you so sorely need to be a real leader.

All of these are tremendously facilitated if you surround yourself with people who don't look like you, don't walk like you, don't talk like you and don't have the same experiences as you do.

Admittedly, when I'm in the US, I'm suddenly diverse. In India, I'm obviously not. But it's not where you come from or what you look like that matters. What matters is what you do and how you do it. That's the true essence of diversity.

What makes diversity so important? Diversity is essential because a group of similar people tends to think in similar ways, reach similar conclusions and have similar blind spots. To guard against that, you need to harness the collective uniqueness of those around you to widen your field of vision—to see things differently, or innovate and to question everything.

Widening that field of vision means widening your worldview, which brings me to my second point around leadership and globality.

2. Leadership and developing a global view

The world is getting smaller and more interdependent than ever, which makes leadership and developing a sense of globality more important than ever. By globality, I mean developing a global view and increasing your connectivity to the world around you. For example, once you get acclimatized to your new jobs, consider getting involved in organizations outside of your work but that connect back to it as well—like a bilateral or a multilateral organization. Explore avenues like the World Economic Forum. There are colleagues of mine at MasterCard who have been very active, even right from their schooldays.

The key is to go beyond looking at the world through the lens of your company or your organization or even your country.

All of which are better served by the mindset that you can't catch the blind spots I just mentioned with blinkers on. Globality is about taking those blinders off. It's about seeing that we've got a global population that's increasing exponentially. We're at seven billion plus today. A hundred years ago, we were at less than two billion. We're expected to reach nine billion in only a few decades. It's about being aware of demographic shifts and what they mean for countries like India and China, where the demographics in both places are moving in opposite directions. It's recognizing that globalization has benefited some but not nearly enough people. In fact, we're seeing some backlash in the form of increased nationalism and, in some cases, chauvinism. It's realizing the role that the world governments and politics play. Who's in and who's out makes a difference in addressing these larger, global concerns. It makes a difference for your company or organization in those countries where it has a presence or wants to have a presence. The regulatory environment around your business will be something you'll want to get a handle on as well.

Globality not only broadens your thinking, it also expands your focus. It enables sectors like government, business, international development, foundations and civil society to get beyond their own spheres—and to coalesce around shared interests or common concerns. I mention all of this because, wherever you're working, as you do your day-to-day tasks, the more you can put what you are doing in a larger, global frame, the more value you will add to those around you—and the more you will deepen an important aspect of leadership.

Globality is the twenty-first century's answer to the ancient Greek ideal of being a citizen of the world. It's the deep appreciation that—in the words of Dr Martin Luther King Jr—'we are all caught in an inescapable network of mutuality . . . whatever affects one directly, affects all indirectly.'

Globality is vital to leadership at any level but it's a prerequisite to leadership at the highest levels, where you will have the greatest opportunities to do well and do good, which brings me to my third point.

3. Why leadership in its highest form facilitates doing well and doing good

Doing well and doing good is an organization or business operating at its very best for itself and for society. It's the highest form of leadership. It's the idea that you can pursue what is in your best interest as well as what is in the interest of others. It's the recognition that your success is tied to the success of others. You know the saying, 'It's lonely at the top'? It's only lonely at the top when you don't bring other people along with you.

This principle of doing well and doing good holds true for any one person or organization, but it's an especially powerful principle for business and the private sector today. In a business sense, it's the idea that the private sector can be a force for growth *and* a force for good. That business can make money *and* make a difference.

As many of you well know, the late C.K. Prahalad, one of the great management thinkers of our time and an IIM Ahmedabad alumnus and former professor here, was a tremendous pioneer and architect around this thinking.

I mention all of this because I believe there's never been a greater opportunity for business to be a force for good in the world. But I also believe that when it comes to this year's graduating class, there's never been a greater opportunity for you, for your generation and mine—to come together, to use the best of what we and the organizations we work for have to offer—all in an effort to meet the global challenges of our time.

To bring more people into the financial mainstream at a time when half the world's adults don't have a bank account; to narrow the widening income inequality gap; to guard against a future where we have the Internet of Everything but not the Inclusion of Everyone; to recognize that women who are half the world can make the whole world better—profoundly better—if just given the same opportunities as men; to realize that the private sector has a role to play in overcoming these challenges but cannot do it alone; that the public sector has a role to play as well but cannot do it alone; and that all of us have a role to play if we put into practice the words of Mother Teresa: 'You can do what I cannot do. I can do what you cannot do. Together, we can do great things.'

Of course, this very school was founded, not just on the idea of public–private partnerships but literally by public–private partnerships. It was the Government of India, the government of Gujarat, local businessmen, Harvard Business School, the Ford Foundation—all coming together, not only to help build industry in India but to help build India itself.

The sun is setting for this evening—but it's rising for India and it's rising for all of you, graduates of 2015. It's rising as you embark on the next leg of your journey. I said at the outset that I didn't have a detailed plan when I graduated. But I did recognize that much had been given to me by my family, my friends and this school, and that these gifts were not ones I wanted to squander. I still feel that sense of obligation to this day. You've got this one precious life to lead as you see fit. All that matters are the limits of your own heart and mind. There are 5,25,600 finite minutes in a given year. You've made every minute count during your time here. No doubt, you will do the same as you move ahead. Make sure you make those minutes count for others as well, as you make your way; that's the essence of leadership. It's the essence of something Mahatma Gandhi once said: 'Individual liberty and interdependence are both essential for life in society. Only a Robinson Crusoe can afford to be all self-sufficient.'

Thank you.

I feel deeply honoured to be invited to deliver the convocation address at this great institute.

Arundhati Bhattacharya

A passionate banker who takes complete ownership and pride in whatever she does and with a career of over thirty-seven years with the State Bank of India (SBI), Arundhati Bhattacharya has many amazing firsts to her name. She is the first woman chairman of the 209-year-old SBI, a Fortune 500 company. She is the only Indian banker featuring in the list of 100 most important active public intellectuals, 'The Leading Global Thinkers of 2014'. She is the only banker to be simultaneously recognized as the Most Powerful Woman in India by *Business Today*, *Forbes Asia* and Bloomberg, apart from being crowned as an outstanding leader by CNBC-TV18. She is the only Indian banker to be on the board of fourteen SBI associates and subsidiaries (including the SBI), six financial institutions and on eleven committees formed by the Government of India to promote country-to-country business initiatives among others. Arundhati is the only public-sector banker to have been awarded EY Entrepreneurial CEO of the Year.

Arundhati joined the SBI in 1977 as a probationary officer (PO), and since then has risen through the ranks to become the chairman of this iconic institution. Under her stewardship, the bank has relentlessly focused on raising risk awareness, assessment, mitigation and monitoring systems. Her other area of particular attention has been technology, where she leads the digital transformation of the bank. This has resulted in multiple new initiatives for extending product ranges and upgrading processes and IT infrastructure. She was also instrumental in the launch of mobile banking in the bank, where the SBI is now a market leader. Interestingly, the SBI is the only bank in India that has rolled out pan-India digital branches till date to offer seamless banking to its customers.

With Arundhati at the helm, the bank has received a record number of twenty-four awards in the last eighteen months, many of which again are firsts to its name. The bank is now the proud recipient of the Best Emerging Market Banks in Asia–Pacific, Best Public Sector Bank, Brand of the Year and the Golden Peacock for Corporate Social Responsibility. to name a few.

As the head of new businesses, Arundhati helped to establish some of the most prominent joint ventures for the bank, including the alliance with the Insurance Australia Group for general insurance, Macquarie for private equity and SocieteGenerale for custodial services. A stint in the SBI's New York office also saw Arundhati overseeing external audit and correspondent relations.

A postgraduate from Jadavpur University, West Bengal, Arundhati is closely associated with various initiatives in the field of education, health and empowering the challenged and differently abled with the aim of integrating them in the society. Soon after assuming the present assignment as chairman, Arundhati has introduced sabbatical leave for women employees to meet their special needs.

Arundhati Bhattacharya

Esteemed Mr Ajit Balakrishnan, chairman, board of governors, IIM Calcutta, Professor Saibal Chattopadhyay, director, IIM Calcutta, members of the board of governors, distinguished guests, faculty and staff members and, above all, the graduating students, their families, friends, respected members of the media, ladies and gentlemen, it is my honour to stand among such eminent people and be a part of the celebration this convocation represents.

Interacting with students and the youth is always an enriching experience—their ideas, their passion and their zeal and willingness to take on challenges are very energizing—and it enthuses us in the firm belief that the future is in capable hands. As you all stand on the cusp of moving on from campus life to the real world, I am sure that there is some amount of apprehension in your minds—it is but natural as you will be moving out of your comfort zones to still-unexplored territory. Like leaving home for campus and hostel life, this is but the next stage of your journey on life's

---

Convocation address delivered by Ms Arundhati Bhattacharya, chairperson, State Bank of India, at the Indian Institute of Management Calcutta, on 5 April 2014. Reproduced with the permission of the author.

curve. I experienced the same tentativeness when I left college to join the SBI and I am sure your seniors have felt the same and so will the future generation. But I am confident that your teachers and mentors, duly supported by your parents and friends, have taught you well and the grooming, the knowledge and the skills imbibed by you all will be infallible tools in helping you face whatever challenges the world has to throw at you. And, believe me, you will make your mark in your chosen fields and make yourself, your institution and your parents proud.

Today's world is one where change is the only constant. We are experiencing this change at every moment. And each change impacts us in various degrees and at various levels. The world is now closely integrated and, like Edward Lorenz's Butterfly Effect (a hurricane's formation being contingent on whether or not a distant butterfly had flapped its wings several weeks earlier), the slightest of changes may impact us in myriad ways. Therefore, preparedness for the unknown is a sine qua non. While you have been suitably tutored on preparedness, I would like to share with you some essential tenets I have gathered from my experience, the three Cs of a winner's checklist, which have continued to give me the strength, conviction and courage to face up to any challenge.

The first of these Cs is creativity. Creativity involves tuning our innovative and imaginative ideas into reality. Creativity is reflected when you see the world in new ways, to perceive the hidden patterns, to establish connectivity between seemingly unrelated phenomena and to generate solutions. In the words of George Bernard Shaw, 'You see things; and you say, "Why?" But I dream things that never were; and I say, "Why not?"'

Creative people have new ideas and new ways of looking at old problems. New ideas mean a willingness to adapt and change and also be a harbinger of change. In the words of Steve Jobs, 'Creativity is just connecting things. When you ask creative people how they did something, they feel a little guilty because they didn't really do it, they just saw something. It seemed obvious to them after a while.'

The question that I am sure must be on your minds now is—can creativity be learned? The short answer is yes. We humans are naturally creative, and creativity is a skill that can be developed and a process that can be managed. Creativity begins with a foundation of knowledge, learning a discipline and mastering a way of thinking. While this institute has provided you with the knowledge and the skill sets, you need to sharpen your ability to look at things in a different dimension. You can do this by provoking unorthodox responses, exploring different ideas and perspectives, questioning assumptions and challenging common wisdom, using imagination to draw connections between unrelated fields.

Creativity makes one grow and gives confidence. More importantly, it keeps boredom away. Ennui and inertia have no place in the life of creative person. The belief that one should be talented and gifted to be creative is a misplaced notion. Creativity is a latent attribute in every individual. No one reached high levels of achievement in their field without devoting thousands of hours to serious training. Mozart trained for sixteen years before he produced an acknowledged masterpiece. In the words of Pablo Picasso, 'Every child is an artist; the problem is staying an artist when you grow up.'

Creativity will give you the ability of problem-solving, having a different perspective to an issue and coming up with differential solutions. I would urge upon you all to make creativity your way of thinking and be imbued with a joie de vivre.

The second C that I place for your consideration is communication. I cannot stress the importance of communication enough. You realize the importance of communication when you play the game of Chinese whispers, in which there is a circle of persons and one person whispers something in his neighbour's ear which gets passed on to the next and so on, and it is always found that the final message is so very different from what was initially communicated. The difference in content and meaning can be very damaging. In the words of Ms Emma Thompson, British actress, screenwriter and author, 'Any problem, big or small, within a family, always seems to start with bad communication. Someone isn't listening.'

Communication is essentially the exchange and flow of information and ideas from one person to another. Communication is effective only when the target group or receiver understands the exact information or idea—both content and context—the sender intends to transmit. This involves active listening, that is, listening with a purpose, understanding body language and non-verbal signals and expressions—these are skills to be learned and acquired if you wish to become an effective leader. Listening is a vital communication skill. When we communicate, we spend

45 per cent of our time listening. Most people take listening for granted, but it is not the same as hearing and should be thought of as a skill. So you, too, must be clear in your communication so that the other person is not left to make his own—often wrong—interpretation with disastrous consequences.

No matter how accomplished one is, ineffective communication can be a big hindrance to progress in life. This is true even in a family situation in which clear communication can diffuse many a problem. Let's take an interview situation or a sales pitch being tuned into what is being expressed by the other party: a candidate or a marketing professional will get all of ten minutes to get his or her point across. Therefore, the ability to communicate can make or mar many a career.

As your career progresses, the importance of communication skills increases; the ability to speak, listen, question and write with clarity and conciseness are essential for most managers and leaders. In the words of Alan Greenspan, American economist and former chairman of the US Federal Reserve, 'To succeed, you will soon learn, as I did, the importance of a solid foundation in the basics of education—literacy, both verbal and numerical, and communication skills.'

Developing your communication skills can help all aspects of your life, from your professional life to social gatherings and everything in between. The ability to communicate information accurately, clearly and as intended is a vital life skill and something that should not be overlooked. It's never too late to work on your communication skills, and, by doing so, improve your quality of life.

In the words of Gilbert Amelio, president and CEO of the National Semiconductor Corporation, 'Developing excellent communication skills is absolutely essential to effective leadership. The leader must be able to share knowledge and ideas to transmit a sense of urgency and enthusiasm to others. If a leader can't get a message across clearly and motivate others to act on it, then having a message doesn't even matter.'

My third and the final C is compassion.

Compassion is one factor that, when practised, brings in long-lasting happiness and fulfilment in one's life. The Dalai Lama, the Buddhist spiritual leader, has stated, 'If you want others to be happy, practise compassion. If you want to be happy, practise compassion.'

Why develop compassion in your life? It helps you to be happier, and brings others around you to be happier. If we agree that it is our common aim to strive to be happy, then compassion is one of the main tools for achieving that happiness. It is, therefore, of utmost importance that we cultivate compassion in our lives and practise compassion every day.

When you help a stranger without a reciprocal motive, it manifests your compassion in action. The principle of compassion transcends all religious, ethical and spiritual traditions. It fosters empathy. It impels us to work tirelessly to ameliorate the suffering of others. Being compassionate has to be instinctive and not compelling. Compassion makes us exalted human beings and fills our lives with joy and happiness. Compassion is limitless and all encompassing. It is not restricted to empathy for fellow human beings—it is much more; it stretches to each and everything in this universe—the environment, the flora and fauna, the living and the nonliving. True compassion is more than an emotional response—it is a commitment to a way of life. Things and work done with compassion are long-lasting and self-sustaining. The main benefit is that it makes you more content and happy and also makes those around you happy. It moves you away from self-centredness to be more outgoing and giving. In the words of Deepak Chopra, New Age guru, 'Enlightened leadership is spiritual if we understand spirituality not as some kind of religious dogma or ideology but as the domain of awareness where we experience values like truth, goodness, beauty, love and compassion, and also intuition, creativity, insight and focused attention.'

To sum up, creativity in generating new and novel ideas, effective communication skills and compassion for others are the set of skills that have helped me in shaping my career and personality. I am sure that as you move forward you will discover your own set of keys and values, which will strengthen and nourish you.

You are all fortunate that you have been endowed with the needed professional skills thanks to this august institution. Successfully graduating is a testimony to your innate talent and higher cognitive abilities. These credentials will ensure a great future for you in terms of material and intellectual enrichment. At the same time, please remember that you owe a lot to society for making you 'privileged citizens'. As such, you have a greater responsibility to pay back society and make it more equitable and harmonious. Contribute your might to serve the nation, make it more inclusive and help in distributing the fruits of development to the dispossessed.

I would like to end my speech with an extract from the Stanford commencement speech made by Steve Jobs in 2005:

> You can't connect the dots looking forward; you can only connect them looking backwards. So you have to trust that the dots will somehow connect in your future. You have to trust in something—your gut, destiny, life, karma, whatever. This approach has never let me down, and it has made all the difference in my life.

I do hope that my talk will help in your new beginning and journey.

My best wishes. God bless!

Thank you.

Shekhar Dutt

Shekhar Dutt was an officer in the Indian Army and was awarded the Sena Medal for Gallantry in the Indo-Pak War in 1971. He then joined the Indian Administrative Service (Madhya Pradesh cadre).

Shekhar Dutt was the Governor of Chhattisgarh from January 2010 to July 2014. Prior to his appointment as Governor, he was India's deputy national security advisor from August 2007 to January 2010 with the responsibility of developing India's strategic defence capabilities.

He has served as Defence Secretary (2005–07) as well as Secretary, defence production (2004–05) in the Government of India. Shekhar Dutt evolved a new defence procurement policy (DPP 2006) and manual (DPM 2006) incorporating the new 'Offset and Make' policies. He led the development of the framework for the US–India defence relationship, and set up a joint Indo-US defence policy group, the new Indo-German defence cooperation, the new Indo-Japanese defence cooperation as well as the new Indo-Australian defence cooperation. He also had the distinction of setting up the first ever defence cooperation agreement with Chile and the Philippines.

As Joint Secretary, ministry of defence (1991–96), Shekhar Dutt served as director on several boards of defence companies such as Bharat Electronics Ltd (BEL), Bharat Earth Movers Ltd (BEML), Mazagaon Dock Ltd (MDL), Garden Reach Ship Builders and Engineers (GRSE), Goa Ship Yard Ltd (GSL) and Bharat Dynamics Ltd (BDL). He was instrumental in setting up the new tank production units at the Ordnance Factory at Avadi and the new BMP production unit at the Ordnance Factory in Medak. He coordinated the Integrated Guided Missile Development Project (IGMDP) from the production side.

As the Principal Secretary, tribal welfare, Government of MP, he introduced special projects providing employment to the tribal forest dwellers. As Principal Secretary, education, sports and youth welfare, he evolved the education guarantee scheme and the 'Shiksha Karmi Bharti Niyam'. Shekhar Dutt has also served as director general, the Sports Authority of India, and Secretary in the health ministry.

Shekhar Dutt

It is my proud privilege to be present here on the occasion of the convocation of the twenty-fifth batch of the postgraduate diploma in forestry management of the Indian Institute of Forest Management (IIFM), Bhopal. This institute has made a mark in the realm of environmental education in the country and has established itself as a catalyst of change in recent years through this course that is a unique blend of management discipline with applications orientation towards environment, forestry and development aspects of natural resource management.

It gives me great pleasure to participate in this ninth convocation ceremony of the IIFM. I congratulate all the students who have successfully completed the course and will be receiving the postgraduate diploma to enter the professional world and assume their responsibilities in the field of environmental management. Today, IIFM's name is an integral part of your identity and, like worthy inheritors of the rich legacy that IIFM has bestowed upon you, you

Convocation address delivered by Shri. Shekhar Dutt, Governor, Chhattisgarh, at the Indian Institute of Forest Management, Bhopal, on 11 April 2014. Reproduced with the permission of the author.

must always carry this legacy with pride and honour. I also congratulate the faculty and staff, who, I am sure, are equally proud of producing these excellent professionals.

We are now passing through a period in which there is a huge stress on the environment, especially in a developing country like India. The need for balancing development with environmental conservation looms large. At this juncture, we need managers who can show us a way of sustainably managing our natural resources and conserving the environment, keeping in mind the immense need of development in our nation. A postgraduate diploma in forestry management has become a very prestigious and sought-after postgraduate diploma, and confers not only immense salary potential but also career advancement. The academic knowledge of the theory and application of business management imparted to you by the institute, when combined with education on environmental and forestry conservation and development, makes an extremely successful natural resource manager out of you. This postgraduate diploma will not only help you propel India's growth and contribute to the global economy, but also help you to ensure conservation, sustainable management and development of the forestry resources of our country for the benefit of the large forest-dependent indigenous population.

India's growth story has been unique in many ways. It has been service sector-driven, consumption-driven and domestically led, with very little external dependencies. It is exactly because of these reasons that the Indian economy was least affected by the global meltdown and could quickly recover from the little setback that it faced. In terms of global competitiveness, India's position is quite paradoxical. In terms of business sophistication, market environment and strength of financial markets, India is ranked very high. But on the other hand, the number of procedures and the time required to start a business in India is very high. Here, too, the one sector that is considered by many as hindering development and speedy clearance to development projects is the forestry and environment sector. Therefore the role of budding environmental and forestry managers like you is extremely important. It is you whose role is ideally cut out to fuel this Indian growth story in a sustainable manner. It is you who will be the harbinger of breaking this myth and will carve out an environmentally sound development path for the future of our country.

With robust growth in all sectors of the economy, increasing globalization and with the market penetrating into sectors hitherto unexploited or restricted to the public sector, there is ample demand for environmental and forestry managers in the Indian economy. Due to limited resources in the public sector, the government is expecting large-scale participation by the private sector in the infrastructure sector, where India is lagging. The Planning Commission has developed standards and guidelines for public–private partnerships, which would be the preferred approach for developing this sector. The government has enacted several laws to make these industries green. The implementation of CSR initiatives by these industries is also obligatory and this is generating a huge demand for educated environmental and forestry managers like you. Therefore, there is a huge demand and ample opportunities for forestry and environmental professionals in the Indian economy and particularly in

Indian companies, where nation-building and your career-building can go hand in hand. Therefore, I would advise you to look beyond the traditional preferences and explore and create new opportunities.

Business ethics and corporate governance are among the most important fundamental principles of business management that I want to emphasize. I am sure you have already studied it as part of your curriculum. This is particularly true for the natural resource management sector in India, where there is a huge controversy in the allotments and unsustainable harvesting of natural resources at the cost of environmental degradation. In our professional life, all of us grapple with the question of what is right and what is wrong on a day-to-day basis. Ethics is not something new to the Indian mind, which has always been obsessed with the concept of dharma, which in essence means doing the right thing. Ethics is nothing but doing the right thing and, in a situation of dilemma or conflict of interest, being able to choose the right path at all costs. Business integrity or ethics is not just about moral or social values but an economic necessity and an essential ingredient for success in business. I would like to warn you that, in several instances in your life, you will be confronted to make decisions to win over a particular situation at the cost of degrading natural resources. I would just request you to relax and give a thought to whether your decision is backed by professional ethics and integrity and whether it is for the general good of our fellow countrymen.

The community-based forest management and small and medium forest enterprises approaches have great potential for sustainable livelihoods. Such enterprises play an important part in the harvesting, processing, transport and marketing of timber and non-timber forest products (NTFPs). Small and medium forest enterprises consist of individual, household and community entrepreneurs as well as associations of actors along the supply chain. For these enterprises, forests and trees are important sources of cash income and employment. They are also important suppliers of many NTFPs, such as bamboo, medicinal plants, forest insects, fruits, nuts and gums and resins. These products are sold in raw, semi-processed and processed forms. The provision of environmental services, such as recreation and ecotourism, is another area in which such enterprises can be gradually more involved. Sustainable small and medium forest enterprises can bring positive economic, social and environmental impacts and make a significant contribution to economic development.

There is increasing concern among people living in and around forests and a realization that they should find a central focus as their livelihood depends on these resources. Further analysis is needed to emphasize the connection between people and forests, and the benefits that can accrue when forests are managed by local people in sustainable and innovative ways through a discussion of traditional knowledge, community-based forest management, small and medium forest enterprises and the non-cash value of forests. These approaches have historically been an essential part of local development, yet our knowledge of their value is still relatively poor.

India has preserved various rare and valuable medicinal plants which can be effectively used for antibacterial, antifungal, anti-amoebic, antimalarial, anti-inflammatory ailments. There is a great scope for commercial cultivation of several medicinal plants in India. We need to identify medicinal plants suitable to our soil and climatic conditions for promoting them among farmers. The farmers and villagers of tribal areas can play a major role in social entrepreneurship initiatives by cultivating different medicinal plants required by pharmaceutical industries. If we wish to move ahead, farmers should be left only to cultivate, while independent organizations should focus on post-harvest processing and storage, together with the network for marketing.

I feel that other than cultivation in their natural habitat, all other activities should, if possible, be integrated for full value addition. Business opportunities in this sector are enormous due to diversified uses of plant-derived molecules and compounds in the pharmaceuticals, nutrition and agri-chemical industries. There is a need to understand the pharmacological aspect of medicinal plants to provide mentoring and support to the export of products derived from medicinal plants. This will encourage our research and development (R & D) organizations and the pharmaceutical industries to discover new bioactive molecules that can be obtained from the medicinal plants and use them to formulate new medicines and drugs; that way, we would be rightfully called a country which is capable of finding innovative products based on solid scientific evidence and principles. We shall then also start owning intellectual property rights (IPR) and wouldn't have to pay royalties on account of international IPR.

The ministry of health along with the Indian Council of Medical Research (ICAR) and the Council of Scientific and Industrial Research (CSIR) decided to collect all our traditional knowledge and its formulas in a digital form and set up a traditional knowledge digital library (TKDL). The TKDL has made it possible that our traditional knowledge cannot be stolen and patented by people who have access to it. Now, this traditional knowledge is our heritage, and only India can hold this right. The time has come when we need to carry on the knowledge acquired and preserved by our ancestors and use it effectively to provide solutions to the health problems of the twenty-first century.

Nowadays, geographic information systems (GIS) significantly enhance the ability to visualize and analyse what is located where and why; it is a vital input for the planning and management of forests. GIS is fast becoming the common integrating element in the implementation of several initiatives in our country that require the participation of forest management planning, implementation and monitoring. These are very useful for forest land and record management, ecotourism development, joint forest planning management (JFPM), sustainable use of natural forests and change and disaster management. An analysis of forest fires can also be augmented by this system.

The complexities of present-day management, with too many uncertain parameters, call for a creative approach to provide innovative solutions to problems. Nowhere is it truer than in natural resource management. As the environment is changing so rapidly in India, you, the new faces of forestry and environment management, need to think out of the box and adapt to the ever-changing field by continuously developing and applying new models to a sustainable natural resource management (NRM). In today's world of competition, the most important competition is between you and your imagination. New approaches should replace the traditional concepts of natural resource management. The societies and nations that had the least resistance to an uninterrupted flow of ideas and concepts have grown faster. I am confident that your young minds will be able to translate new ideas into practical approaches of balancing development with sustainable natural resource management. Experience has shown that home-grown, localized solutions to problems have proved more effective than importing ideas from elsewhere. Hence, local traditional knowledge, especially in the remote forest states and districts of our country, mostly inhabited by indigenous people, if adopted with suitable contemporary modifications, will prove to be more sustainable and effective than solutions imposed externally. Hence, go out in this world and build a niche for yourself as dynamic, creative, confident young minds who have the ability to counter all the hardships that presently loom large over the management of the NRM sector not only in India but the world as a whole.

I would like to close my address with these famous words of Albert Einstein: 'Out of clutter find simplicity; from discord find harmony; in the middle of difficulty lies opportunity.'

When I look ahead, I see a very bright future for IIFM and its students. Your institution stands on a vast array of opportunities that can open limitless possibilities for your academic growth. IIFM will have to ensure that it meets societal aspirations by providing leadership through cutting-edge research, providing useable knowledge and direction to the industry and the government alike. It should aggressively aim and strive to become the number one institution in the world in its knowledge domain.

I would like to once again congratulate all the students, wishing them a fulfilling life and a very successful career. I would also like to congratulate IIFM and its faculty for the wonderful work they have been doing and also for giving me this opportunity to be present here today. I wish you all a very successful career ahead and a very satisfying professional life.

Thank you.

Jai Hind.

R. Gopalakrishnan

R. Gopalakrishnan (Gopal to his friends) studied physics at St Xavier's, Kolkata, engineering at the Indian Institute of Technology Kharagpur and attended the advanced management programme at the Harvard Business School. He is a former president of the All India Management Association.

He retired from executive positions in the Tata company in 2011. Currently, Gopal is a non-executive director of Tata Group parent, Tata Sons and several Tata companies. He also serves as an independent director of listed companies, Akzo Nobel India, Castrol India and Hemas, Sri Lanka.

Gopal has been a professional manager from 1967: thirty-one years in Unilever and seventeen years in Tata. Over the last twenty-five years, he has served in Jeddah as chairman of Unilever Arabia, in Bangalore as managing director of Brooke Bond Lipton and vice chairman of Hindustan Lever, and in Mumbai as executive director of Tata Sons.

Gopal advises companies and mentors leaders as the president of Mindworks. He also speaks extensively and writes thought pieces.

He is actively engaged in both instructional and inspirational speaking and is represented by an international agency. He has spoken at many events in the last four years—Hong Kong, Hangzhou, Kuala Lumpur, Colombo, Dubai, Abu Dhabi, Brussels (Liege), Paris and Philadelphia. He also speaks extensively within India. His subjects have been in the areas of governance, strategy, organizational transformation, people management, innovation, markets and India. His speeches and workshops are based on practical examples; they tend to be anecdotal rather than rich in theory or based on analytical frameworks.

He has taught an unusual course titled 'LWNT: Learning What's Not Taught' at B-schools.

He has written many articles in newspapers. He has authored four bestselling books; some of them have been translated into Chinese, Hindi and Tamil.

R. Gopalakrishnan
(Kashipur, 17 March 2015)

At this convocation, I wish to focus upon only two messages. First, it is good to be angry, a sort of positive anger. Second, it is not good to ever lose hope.

Being angry

In August 1765, the descendant of Emperor Aurangzeb signed and handed over a scroll to an Englishman called Robert Clive. There is a painting by Benjamin West in the British Museum to mark this occasion. The scroll handed over to the East India Company gave away the Mughal emperor's right to collect all the taxes in Bengal, Bihar and Orissa. These territories had been won by the British from Siraj ud-Daulah after Robert Clive had bribed army chief Mir Jafar to let the English win the war (nowadays we call this match-fixing). The painting shows Emperor Shah Alam sitting at a height and bending at the waist as he hands over

---

Convocation address delivered by Mr R. Gopalakrishnan, director of Tata Sons Ltd, at the Indian Institute of Management Kashipur, on 17 March 2015. Reproduced with the permission of the author.

the scroll to an imperious-looking and upright Robert Clive. The genuflection at the waist certainly appears to suggest a position of weakness in the postures.

In that case, the ruler bowed down to a businessman for, after all, Robert Clive was a mere officer of the East India Company. In a role reversal, since Independence, Indian businessmen have regularly bowed down to the new rulers—ministers, MPs and bureaucrats. My first advice to you is that, during your management career, never kowtow to anyone in power. You don't need to be arrogant, but you should never have to be subservient either. Always do an honest piece of professional management work, be proud of your contribution to society and be slightly angry about wanting to do more. The results that can be achieved by being slightly angry are illustrated by three key events by India as a nation.

- 1965: The green revolution—national response under duress of the PL 480 cessation—the four Ss being Lal Bahadur Shastri, C. Subramanaiam, Dr M.S. Swaminathan and Food Secretary S. Shivaraman.
- 1971: The white revolution—national response in the face of acute milk shortage despite having the world's largest bovine population—Operation Flood led from the front by Dr V. Kurien
- 1991: The supercomputer revolution—C-DAC response to the US's denial of Cray supercomputer technology after India tested a nuclear device at Pokhran, led by Dr Vijay Bhatkar—the launch of the world's second-fastest supercomputer, PARAM, at the Zurich Supercomputing Show in 1991—*Washington Post* greeted the event with the headline 'Angry India does it again'.

In short, constructive anger is good. I wish you a career of constructive anger if India is to progress.

Hope and despair

We Indians seem to periodically have a sense of gloom and doom with respect to India's situation. 'Has India blown it?' many people ask. I find myself struggling, both for words as well as the time to express my thoughts. So I felt I would use this opportunity to view the subject rationally rather than emotionally.

The expression 'blow it' literally means 'to spoil your chances' or 'to lose an opportunity'. So the questions I address are:

- Has India lost an opportunity and, if so, over what time frame?
- Did other nations also blow it?
- What are the simple indicators?

Time frame

The time frame over which you judge the question is important. Time is relative; it is what is perceived by the viewer.

For example, even though you move your folded newspaper at great speed to swat a fly, the fly escapes with alacrity and speed. Why? Because the fly's eye has a different CFF compared to the human eye. CFF stands for critical fusion frequency and is the frequency at which a flicker stands still. Humans have a CFF of sixty cycles per second, while flies have a CFF five times higher—250 cycles per second.

This means that, to the fly, your speed comes through as five times slower than how you perceive it. A fly-eye view of an F1 racing driver is that of a comfortable weekend driver, cruising through a country road. That is why your rapidly moving folded newspaper is perceived by the fly to be as slow as a wooden spoon moving through honey or treacle.

When you review the progress of a vast nation or society like India, there has to be some perspective of time, to use an appropriate CFF factor. It cannot just be last week's Sensex or the next month's *Mann Ki Baat* talk.

To emphasize the importance of the time perspective, imagine that you are examining the proposition 'Sachin Tendulkar has blown it'. If you disagree with the proposition, you will find plenty in the full cricketing career of the iconic player to prove your point. But if you were to review only his last twenty Test matches and compare his performance with his peers in their last twenty Test matches, here is what you would find:

- Sachin's score of 1070 runs in 33 innings ranks last among Brian Lara, Rahul Dravid, V.V.S. Laxman and Ricky Ponting, whose run scores are in the range of 1128–1953.
- Sachin's per innings average is 33 runs, against his peers' averages of 34–53 runs.
- In his last twenty Test matches, Sachin's highest score was 94, whereas his peers scored 176–226 runs each.
- In their last twenty Test matches, his peers scored two to eight centuries each, but Sachin scored zero centuries.

So did Sachin blow it? If you review only his last and recent performance, the answer is yes. But that is not true, you all know it! It is important to have a perspective of time.

Comparisons

Therefore, I reviewed India's progress—or the lack of it—over the thirteen years of the new millennium. This has the added advantage that it covers an NDA [National Democratic Alliance] as well as a UPA [United Progressive Alliance] period. I also benchmarked with non-China BRICS [Brazil, Russia, India, China and South Africa] economies like Brazil and Indonesia to make the comparisons as relevant as possible. Please note that I am reviewing the country, not the UPA or the NDA.

I compared IMF data on the acceleration of annual GDP growth between the last thirteen years of the old millennium (1986–99) with thirteen years of the New Millennium (1999–2012). Europe decelerated by 102 basis points; Indonesia accelerated by just 10 basis points; and Brazil added 95 basis points. But India added 120 basis points, second only to China. [A basis point is one-hundredth of a percentage point.]

Urbanization is a good driver of economic growth. Since 1991, Indian urbanization grew by 250 basis points per year, matched by Indonesia, but both countries were far ahead of Brazil, which grew at half the rate at 120 points. India is urbanizing like a bullet train.

In the new millennium, India's real annual growth rate of disposable income advanced at a whopping 650 basis points, compared to Indonesia at 400 and Brazil at 360. In the new millennium, India's ranking in agricultural production improved enormously.

In the new millennium, India has emerged as the number one global producer of milk and fruits, the number two global producer of vegetables, cotton, wheat and sugarcane. India has surpassed Thailand as the number one rice exporter in the world.

India's production of passenger cars grew in the new millennium by 1500 basis points per year, compared to the Asia-Pacific region's 1200 and Brazil's 700.

The growth track record over the post-Independence period is as follows.

Period	Real GDP growth (%)	Population growth (%)	Real per capita income growth (%)	Comments
1951–52 to 1979–80	3.5	2.2	1.3	Post-Independence initial year
1980–81 to 1991–92	5.2	2.1	3.1	Pre-reform
1992–93 to 2000–01	6.1	2.0	4.1	Immediate post-reform
2001–02 to 2010–11	7.6	1.6	6.0	Current period

India's per capita income changes

So we have experienced the best thirteen years in our five-thousand-year history, and what do we do? We perpetually debate whether India has blown it! Rather odd!

Would you treat the serious business of economic and social progress of 1.2 billion people by the yardsticks of cricket, where a batsman is judged by his last few innings?

For sure, in the last few years, the same indices that I have quoted declined compared to the immediate past period. There has undoubtedly been some effect of the global downturn. To use the tennis metaphor, you cannot compare grass court tennis with clay court tennis. As the world economy has become more VUCA in the last five years—volatile, uncertain, complex and ambiguous—India retained its position at number two among the fastest-growing nations. It is worthwhile to note that when the tide rose in the first eight years of the new millennium, India accelerated and improved its position.

My audience might think that I have conveniently avoided talking about China. For many centuries, the Chinese economy has been bigger than India in total money terms. In per capita terms, China and India had the same per capita income in 1970. Today, admittedly, China has three times what India has on this measure. However, bear in mind that if Indians had, in the 1970s, let Sanjay Gandhi implement his measures to limit the Indian family size (as China had done), the per capita income of China would not be three times India's but only one and a half times!

Although China liberalized thirteen years before India, India's per capita GDP lags behind China by only eight years, and in per capita private consumption, India lags behind China by only by five years. India's per capita consumption of steel, cement, soda ash, soaps and many others—all lag behind China and the developed economies by a factor of 10–50 per cent.

The headroom for growth should send anybody in a tizzy; it is unbelievable.

You have to view all this data as an opportunity rather than as a problem. In that case you will get blown away by India rather than debate whether India has blown it!

Corruption

I should add a brief word about corruption, which is undoubtedly a distressing feature of India. Without accepting it as a necessary evil, I would respectfully point out that corruption is like a virus. It affects society and its effects are disastrous. Every society has to keep vaccinations as a preventive and medicines as a curative. India is no exception.

But let us not forget that though India is a 5000-year-old civilization, it is only twenty-two years old in its incarnation as a capitalist democracy. When other countries were at a similar phase in their development—the US, the UK, Korea, Taiwan—history tells us that they faced similar crises. The British Parliament would not have despaired about its bleak future in 1893, nor would Teddy Roosevelt have done so for America in 1906.

Switzerland is generally regarded as a clean, corruption-free economy. Considering that it has recycled into dignity Nazi money, dirty money from African politicians and black money from Indian businessmen, it qualifies as the world's biggest hawala operator. Is it right to place it on top of Transparency International's ratings? It is worth pondering the subject.

So does all this mean that India has seized every opportunity and missed none? No, of course not. Life is all about missing many opportunities, but grabbing some others. The issue is whether you are grabbing your opportunities well enough compared to others in a competitive sense.

And India has done exactly that.

At the equivalent stage of India's current economic development, Britain took 170 years, from 1700 to 1871, to double its per capita income; America took fifty years, from 1832 to 1882. India, at the recent growth rates, since 1996, doubled its per capita income in fourteen years.

The Economist ran a lead piece in 2013 titled 'Has Brazil blown it'? The magazine mourned the fact that Brazil's growth, which peaked at 7.5 per cent per annum in 2009, had collapsed to below 1 per cent. Now *that* seems more like blowing it!

As a citizen, I would have liked India to grab more opportunities. But I can, with sobriety, think of many opportunities I have failed to grab during my career and life. But I would staunchly refute any suggestion that, with respect to my life, I have 'blown it'.

The nation just needs its citizens—young people, entrepreneurs and businessmen—to have the confidence that

India will recover soon. This requires acceptance from the political leadership that a new action agenda is required. This possibility is a real one.

The greatest obstacle to a recovery is having a population that does not expect it! I hope young people do not despair. If that happens, then I am sure that India would surely have blown it!

R. Gopalakrishnan

(Udaipur, 21 March 2015)

The economic environment

Our country is going through uncertain times, as happens with every society periodically. If you watch TV or read the newspapers, you could get depressed. The problem does not lie with the times we live in or with the media. The solution lies in your perspective. You have the choice to think differently. If I have a single message for you, it is this: your generation is poised to escort the country into its most prosperous phase. Live your life with positive energy.

It is human nature to want to know the future, but nobody knows it. The view of the so-called experts is no more reliable than if chimpanzees were to throw darts at a dartboard. History is littered with failed prophecies.

- In 1877, Western Union Company stated, 'The telephone has too many shortcomings to be considered as a means of communication and is inherently of no value to our company.'

Convocation address delivered by Mr R. Gopalakrishnan, director of Tata Sons Ltd, at the Indian Institute of Management Udaipur, on 21 March 2015. Reproduced with the permission of the author.

- In 1899, Charles Duell of the US patent office stated, 'everything that can be invented has been invented'.
- On 8 January 1913, Netaji Subhas Chandra Bose wrote a letter to his elder brother: 'Is our dear country on the high road to progress? India is wading through sin and corruption but as the eye of prudence, prophecy or foresightedness can behold, all is darkness.'
- In 1943, IBM founder Thomas Watson said, 'I think that there is a world market for computers of maybe five computers.'
- In his 1968 book, Stanford biologist Paul Ehrlich declared that 'the battle to feed all of humanity is over'.
- International Monetary Fund economist Prakash Loungani commented about economists that 'the record of failure to predict recessions is virtually unblemished.'

So do not get trapped by the so-called experts. Consider your inheritance and live life responsibly and king-sized. As you inherit, please remember that you too need to be good ancestors. Enrich the society you will live in as you develop your career and leave an even better India for your children.

For the students who are graduating, this is a wonderful day. Your teachers have nurtured you professionally, as indeed your parents and elders have nurtured you personally over several years. These are acts to be grateful for. I recall a memorable metaphor from nature:

Many species of animals undertake some form of protecting to help their young adjust to their new environment. But there are exceptions. Science writers say that, unlike mammals and humans, reptiles have no emotion. They mate, drop their eggs and simply walk away. It is known to be true of many species of snakes, turtles and so on. However, the crocodile is an interesting case.

When the eggs are ready for hatching, the mother crocodile digs them out of the nest and gently cracks the eggshell to let the young ones out. The young ones are very vulnerable to predators. The mother gathers the babies into the pouched floor of her mouth—not to eat them, as is erroneously assumed, but to protect her young ones. She then heads for the river close by. Upon entering the water, she opens her jaws to release the young into the water.

Your teachers have behaved like the mother crocodile—they have held you all in the protective environment of their pouches for a few years and are about to release you into the swirling and threatening waters of the real world today.

Congratulations to you and always remember that you owe them a debt of gratitude.

This wonderful institute has provided you one 'I' in the form of 'instruction'. What you need in your professional life is another 'I' for 'intuition' and a third 'I' for 'inspiration'.

I wish to share five lessons to support this point of view.

Develop intuition by learning what cannot be taught

It is good to always remember that your professional goal is not to be just knowledgeable, but also to be wise.

Knowledge comes from learning what can be taught. Intuition is learning what cannot be taught. Wisdom is a combination of the two.

Anything that can be taught (like science, economics and management) can be learnt by studying at suitable institutions. When institutes teach techniques and concepts, they appeal to the analytical part of the student's brain. The graduating student feels that he or she knows a lot about management, but this is only partly true. Real-life practice is much more than the acquisition of such knowledge or a degree. All of you have to learn many other things which cannot be taught. Management principles are tenets, at best philosophies, but certainly not discoveries in any scientific sense.

A great manager realizes that the energy to manage actually comes from the dark side. It comes from everything that makes him suffer: difficult trade unions, unreasonable competitors, change-resistant middle managers, poor top teams and so on. As he struggles against these negative powers, he is forced to live more deeply, more fully.

A great manager is someone who has realized that he or she is mortal, that is, he or she can make mistakes, that he or she will not be in that job or position in a few years. This is what makes him or her develop compassion for others.

A manager can develop to his or her full potential by learning to be intuitive, inclusive and humane—the kind of skills that are not *taught*. Intuition is not a substitute for analytics and formal learning. It is a winning overlay; it complements knowledge.

Follow your compass, not your clock

We live in the Blackberry and Internet age. Time is the most precious commodity, and just about everyone is short of it.

I call this act of living a time-challenged existence as is the clock.

When we use our time, we do those things that we like to do and avoid the others. Some people have the time to read books but not socialize. Others have the time to attend parties, but not to write letters to friends or exercise to keep fit. All of them are busy.

In organizations, an atmosphere gets built up without anybody's design or desire. This atmosphere pressures managers to give time to the organization—time becomes the surrogate measure for the employee's commitment. In reality, commitment is measured not by the time one gives to the company but by the energy and mind space one gives.

Time is out of our control and, anyway, we suffer from limitations on how much we give to the organization. Rather than try to control the time we give to the organization, we would achieve greater success if we tried to control the energy we give to the organization. You can control your energy by thinking about your 'purpose'.

Each of us has a 'purpose', a compass. Each one's purpose is uniquely personalized, unarticulated and internalized. Purpose is crucial in society for three reasons: it is the primary source of achievement; it is the core energy that fuels the human dynamic; and it is what successful leaders try to keep activated.

There is, however, one dimension of purpose which is universal to all human beings—people want something out of their work so that their lives mean something; they want their lives to have a reason. Fulfilment and happiness come out of working to your potential, irrespective of whether you are a doorman or a chairman.

That is why purpose is a function of character, because you notice it by its absence. To be effective, purpose must be based on a moral idea, by which I mean that it concerns itself with valuing some types of human activities over others.

It is this compass or purpose that makes a lawyer give up his successful practice and fight for the independence of his country as Gandhiji or Nehruji did. It is this compass or purpose that makes a government officer or soldier go beyond the call of his duty, or a company to uplift the society around it through CSR. It is purpose that makes GE a lean machine of efficiency and Google an innovative outfit.

As you work in management, you will be under pressure to follow your clock. Stop and reflect occasionally to ask whether you are following your compass as well. That alone can provide meaning to your life.

Immerse yourself in your profession

The manifestation of 'giving energy' is to immerse yourself in your chosen profession. Immersion means experiencing emotions and involvement so deeply that the lessons enter your brain's remote memory. When needed, these lessons pop up on your mental screen without your trying. Achieving total immersion is a key step in the management of your energy and the development of intuition. Travelling, talking to customers and staying rooted mentally and emotionally are all ways of doing so.

You may enjoy listening to this true story about a famous film star of the 1940s and 1950s—Leela Chitnis.

Leela was the antithesis of a film star. She was the skinny and gawky daughter of a professor; she wore thick glasses. She fell in love with Dr Gajanand Chitnis, who was fourteen years older, a Marathi editor and playwright by occupation. They had a couple of children, but the family income needed augmenting. So Leela started to accompany her husband to rehearsals, and helped with the costumes and sets in order to earn a bit of money. She observed all the goings-on, evening after evening, in a complete emotional involvement. One evening the lead female star failed to turn up. Leela was thrust on the stage only because she had attended endless rehearsals.

Now, from the recesses of her brain, she dredged up the dialogues. She became a star overnight. In 1940, when Lux soap sought Indian girls as models for the first time, Leela was chosen. Thereafter, there was no looking back.

Such is the value of immersion—and chance!

Work incessantly on managing your derailers

I will narrate the situation of a very pure and old monkey species called the vervet—perhaps Hanuman was a vervet. These vervets act exceptionally cleverly under some circumstances. For example, vervets can give three different signals to communicate three different types of predators. Yet, in another circumstance, they act very stupidly—if they see a carcass, they will not suspect that a predator may be around and they will approach the carcass with all the mischief and curiosity of a monkey.

Managers are like vervet monkeys.

Business books and magazines are full of stories about highly intelligent and extremely successful CEOs who suddenly seem to act in a silly way. In management, we are taught about talent management, performance appraisals and accelerating top performers. If such systems work quite well, why do we see CEOs being fired? After all, they have been appraised and watched for several years and must be having excellent reports to their credit if they have reached the position of CEO. And one fine day, he is worthy of being fired?

In my experience, there are three reasons that account for this strange occurrence. The first is that a manager's intelligence is contextual, which means that signals that he or she picks up in one situation may not be picked up in another situation. The second is that power reduces a person's ability to reflect. The third is that he or she overestimates the value of his or her own solutions due to insularity or arrogance.

As you develop your career, you will realize that you are prone to some weaknesses that are uniquely personal to you; for example, short temper, arrogance, garrulousness, insensitivity and so on. These are called derailers. It is very difficult to completely remove such weaknesses, but you can push yourself to a heightened awareness of your derailers. In this way, you can reduce their damage potential.

It is not so well known that the Ramayana character Ravana was a well-read and learned person. In fact, Ravana had undertaken such severe austerities that the gods appeared before him and granted him a special boon. He asked that his death should not come from a god, demon or animal. He did not include a human being in his wish as he just could not imagine that a frail human could ever kill him. Ultimately, he was slain by a human.

In Mexico, the Aztecs ruled successfully during the sixteenth century. They were highly advanced in the arts and sciences, but they were blinded by a deeply religious belief that, one day, their founding god would reappear in a different form. When the Spanish conqueror Hernán Cortés appeared in 1519 at their border, the Aztecs thought that he was the returning god. In spite of a number of contrary signals, Cortés was received with gifts and warmth right up to the emperor, Montezuma. On 13 August 1519, the Aztecs surrendered and the Spanish ruled them for over three hundred years.

How could such an intelligent Ravana or such a successful emperor as Montezuma do such stupid things to cause their own downfall?

They forgot to manage their derailers.

Success is a thief; failure is a fortune

Success is a thief. That is why success is not something to be pursued. This thief brings only unhappiness to those who pursue it. The best chance of capturing this elusive thing called success is to look within us. It may be hiding, but it is right there! However, almost all of the 6.5 billion people on earth try looking for success outside of them.

The problem is that they think of success in others' context. That is why they relentlessly pursue the acquisition of things that others can readily see—wealth, status and recognition. Such success is a thief.

A thief has three characteristics: first, a thief is not recognized by you as being a thief; second, he robs you of what you have without your realizing it at the time; and third, a thief leaves you feeling very foolish after you have been robbed.

So it is with success. You assume that visible symbols of success make you happy, but such success increases the chances that you will be robbed of your happiness, and further, after losing your happiness, you feel foolish that you have lost your success.

Consider the reality around us. A consulting and accounting firm called KPMG conducted a fraud survey in 2008 among the largest private and public companies. An incredible 80 per cent opined that fraud is a problem. To those who doubt the concerns about ubiquitous fraud, further evidence comes from the Satyam episode, which has hogged newsprint and airwaves for the last several weeks.

Charles Michael Schwab was born in 1862. At the age of thirty-five, he became president of US Steel, later Carnegie Steel. He was big, rich and famous. He built an ambitious seventy-five-room private house, Riverside, for $7 million. He lost all his wealth in the 1929 crash and died in 1939 with a debt of $300,000.

Howard Hopson was born in 1882. By the early 1920s, he put together AGECO, an association of electric and gas companies in New York, Ohio and Pennsylvania. He then indulged in what turned out to be shenanigans. He faced trial in 1940 and died in the Brooklyn sanatorium.

All of these 'successful' people lost the perspective of context.

The plain fact is that success has to be seen within a context, and that context is your own self, not outside of yourself. Strip away the context and you see it completely differently.

To most of mankind, success means having wealth and status, which others can be impressed with. But the trick of showing something is not to retain it. The blue object looks blue because the object sends back the blue wavelength of light and retains none of it. Similarly, a successful person returns success and retains none of it.

Just as the Himalayan musk deer tires itself out by running around seeking the source of the fragrance, little realizing that the smell originates from its own navel, man too, should search his own self.

I am not sure who wrote this line but it is wonderful: 'It is not what you gather, but what you scatter that tells what kind of life you have lived.'

Conclusion

I have shared just five lessons that I have learned; I could go on for a long time. But these lessons are not taught, they are learnt by you. I wish you luck in learning what you cannot be taught. Enjoy the journey and my best wishes are with you. God bless.

A.P.J. Abdul Kalam

Dr A.P.J. Abdul Kalam was born and raised on the island of Rameshwaram, in the state of Tamil Nadu at the southern tip of India. His passion for learning led him from humble beginnings to the prestigious Madras Institute of Technology, where he became an aeronautical engineer.

After a brief stint at the Defence Research and Development Organization of India (DRDO), Dr Kalam joined the Indian Space Research Organization (ISRO), where he became the project director for India's first Satellite Launch Vehicle (SLV-3) which placed the satellite Rohini in orbit.

Later, he rejoined the DRDO and played a pivotal role in the development of India's ballistic missile systems and eventually rose to be the scientific adviser to the Defence Minister of India. Dr Kalam was appointed later as principal scientific adviser to the Government of India, in the rank of a cabinet minister, where he was involved in the policy and strategic decisions in transforming

India into a developed nation and a nuclear weapons state. Dr Kalam holds the post of chancellor of the Indian Institute of Space Science and Technology and distinguished professor of many academic institutions.

However, his technological contributions also extend to the biomedical area, where his expertise in materials led to collaboration with medical specialists in the development of low-weight orthosis calipers and a cost-effective cardiac stent.

Dr Kalam is passionate about transforming society through technology, in particular by inspiring the youth of India to harness science and technology for human welfare. During the last ten years he has met more than seventeen million youth across the nation.

Dr Kalam is the recipient of many national and international awards including honorary doctorates from forty-eight universities from India and abroad. He received the Bharat Ratna in the year 1997. Widespread recognition, coupled with his extensive government service, made Dr Kalam a popular choice for high office, and he became the eleventh President of India for a five-year term in 2002–07. His popularity has endured, and he is still affectionately called the People's President for bridging the gap between high office and the common people.

In addition to the autobiography *Wings of Fire*, Dr Kalam has written several books and most of them are household names.

A.P.J. Abdul Kalam

I am delighted to participate in the twenty-eighth annual convocation of the T.A. Pai Management Institute here in this beautiful university town. I congratulate the graduating students for their academic performance and the faculty members for shaping the young minds who are going to be a vital resource in all our national development missions. My greetings to the parents and the audience.

During the last three decades, TAPMI, a member of the Manipal Group of Institutions, has graduated into a very large institution, with over 3000 MBA graduates. I am happy that this institution ranks as one of the best in the nation and is among the institutions to have received the global accreditation by the Association to Advance Collegiate Schools of Business (AACSB). I was reading about the activities on campus, and I was particularly happy to read about the student initiative called JoyFest—an initiative of the social endeavour group of TAPMI—to involve management students in teaching underprivileged children around the campus. Such a process

---

Convocation address delivered by Dr A.P.J. Abdul Kalam, former President of India, at the T.A. Pai Management Institute, Manipal, on 2 April 2014. Reproduced with the permission of the author.

of human sensitivity is indeed the need of the next generation of business leaders.

I congratulate the pioneers, both present and past, who have continuously strived to maintain the standards of the university. The university is a vital part of the development pattern of the nation. Hence, the topic I have selected for discussion today is 'A sustainable development system for the nation'.

Friends, throughout my professional life, I have perceived the impact of a confluence of minds. While managing the SLV-3, the integrated guidance missile development programme or working on India vision 2020, I realized how enquiring and committed minds with a mission focus produced dramatic results. Of all resources, the ignited mind of the youth is the most powerful, on the earth, above the earth and under the earth. What I am most happy is that many youngsters of such programmes are today occupying leading positions in many complex national ventures. Vision, missions and complex problems need and create creative leaders.

Combating economic turbulence through global enterprises

In the recent scenario of global economic turbulence, in both the US and Europe, I reflected on the question, 'Is a new global system emerging?' Many recent events came to my mind. All of you are aware of how scientists from India and the US had been receiving valuable data from their payloads being flown in India's Chandrayaan satellite, which had been successfully placed into earth orbit and then to lunar orbit through complex orbital manoeuvres. In a unique partnership between India and Russia, the supersonic BrahMos missile has been realized and is available for both the countries and for the global market. We have seen how the world specialists were with the Indian agricultural scientists, administrators and farmers, when they brought about the first green revolution and they continue to engage in discussions to meet the current challenges. Today, major Indian software firms and many entrepreneurs from India are part of the software progress of the world. In the manufacturing sector, we hear Indian companies are acquiring companies from other parts of the world. We are seeing how the world's leaders are valuing India's opinion as a champion of South Asia on both regional and global issues.

When I was travelling in an aircraft in the US, I was told that much of its controls were software-driven and most probably developed in India. When I presented my credit card, I was told that it was being processed in the back-end server located in Mauritius. When I walked into a software development house in Bengaluru, I was fascinated to find that it truly presented a multicultural environment. A software developer from China, a project leader from Korea, a software engineer from India, a hardware architect from the US and a communication expert from Germany, all working together to solve a banking problem in Australia.

What message do we get from these events and many such occurrences in the past decade? Do they not indicate a new world order is emerging? Technology has made the world come together. For the past few months, I had several opportunities to meet with world specialists, economists and leaders in India, Israel, the UK, the US and other countries.

The outcome of the discussions led to interesting possibilities for taking education forward in a 'borderless world'. During my last visit to the UK, I addressed the World Youth Congress, where I interacted with youths from many countries. Irrespective of nativity, there was a resonance in thinking, 'How are we going to live in a peaceful and prosperous world?' We in India are working for a developed India by 2020 with concrete integrated action plans in various areas. I am sure the experience gained from one-sixth of the global population will be valuable for the entire world.

Let me now talk about the current state of the national economy.

Current ambience

India is today the third-largest economy in terms of GDP. The Indian economy was growing at an average of 9 per cent per annum till 2009. Then, following the US-originated crisis, the Indian economy had been affected due to global economic turbulence; nevertheless it grew at about 7 per cent in 2009. In 2010, the GDP growth once again started reaching 9 per cent. Then, in 2011, again with the Europe-originated crisis adding on to the turbulence, the economy slowed down but nevertheless grew at about 6.9 per cent. The slowdown became more pronounced in 2012 and 2013, partially attributed to the currency rate crisis, and the economy grew at 4.7 per cent and 4.5 per cent in 2012 and 2013, respectively.

Two trends emerge here. First, India is a resilient economy when it comes to its dependence on external factors—as shown in 2008–10. However, the Indian economy has its own domestic factors of dependence, largely due to trade deficits, which can undermine growth rates.

I was asking myself, what type of innovation is needed to enrich the Indian economy in the present circumstances? I had discussions on this subject with many experts. It came to light that the Indian economy will be less affected due to the global financial crisis originating in the US and Europe. This is because (i) the liberalization process in India has its checks and balances consistent with the unique social requirements of the country, (ii) the Indian banking system has always been conservative, which had prevented the crisis, and (iii) the Indian psyche is generally savings-oriented and living within one's means is part of the mindset. However, at the same time, India's trade deficit, which is the excess of imports over exports, is a matter of concern; last year, it stood at $190 billion. The major factor behind this is the cost of importing crude oil—about $170 billion, or around 87 per cent of the total trade deficit—followed by the import of gold.

Importance of technological innovation

This is the time when technological innovation has to be encouraged in our thinking to rejuvenate in particular the agricultural and rural sectors, through value addition, and to get the small and medium-scale industries and enterprises to contribute a greater share to GDP. I foresee possibilities of creating new markets through rural potential and employment giving rise to interesting possibilities of public–private–community partnerships and international partnerships. Above all, we need effective policy alignments to suit the conditions. Also, the scientists and technologists have to work in appropriate region-specific rural technologies to transform India's rural sector into a vibrant socioeconomic entity. This should spur exports and reliance on non-oil imports.

Another area which needs to be pursued is energy independence—freedom from fossil fuels—by setting a mission mode programme in hydro, solar, nuclear, biofuels and wind power. We need to set a 100 per cent energy independence target by the year 2030 to create an economy which is not burdened by the weight of our energy demands.

Now, let me give my visualization of India during the year 2020.

- A nation where the rural and urban divide has reduced to a thin line.
- A nation where there is an equitable distribution of and adequate access to energy and quality water.
- A nation where the agriculture, industry and service sectors work together in symphony.
- A nation where education with a value system is not denied to any meritorious candidates because of societal or economic discrimination.
- A nation which is the best destination for the most talented scholars, scientists and investors.
- A nation where the best of healthcare is available to all.
- A nation where governance is responsive, transparent and corruption-free.
- A nation where poverty has been totally eradicated, illiteracy removed and crimes against women

and children are absent and none in the society feel alienated.

- A nation that is prosperous, healthy, secure, devoid of terrorism, peaceful and happy and continues along a sustainable growth path.
- A nation that is one of the best places to live in and is proud of its leadership.

To achieve this distinctive profile of India, we have the mission of transforming India into a developed nation. We have identified five areas where India has core competency for integrated action:

1. Agriculture and food processing
2. Education and healthcare
3. Information and communication technology
4. Reliable and quality electric power, surface transport and infrastructure for all parts of the country
5. Self-reliance in critical technologies

These five areas are closely interrelated and, progressing in a coordinated way, will lead to food, economic and national security and achieving energy independence.

Changing business world

Friends, I understand many of you would be joining some of the best corporations of the nation and abroad. I am also sure that some of you today, and some in the future, will start up your own enterprises in different fields. I have some observations for you, as managers and entrepreneurs, of three new business trends which are emerging in the twenty-first century.

First, there is going to be the challenge of facing a new consumer. Experts estimate that developing economies could account for 60 per cent of the new consumption growth in the next years—a potential $15 trillion opportunity. This opportunity would reside in China, India, Brazil, Mexico, Turkey and Russia. Understanding and predicting the needs of these new consumers, their price sensitivities and so on, will be critical for businesses to thrive. Simple, well-catered products, often online, such as WhatsApp, are going to grow into $19 billion valuations, starting from scratch, within a period of less than a decade.

Second, there is going to be a trend of new expectations. What worked yesterday might not work today and will almost definitely fail tomorrow. There will be no such concept of stable businesses, and the corporations of tomorrow will be dynamic, evolving and constantly improving, following the Japanese management concept of kaizen. Consumers expect not only better and reliable services, but also that businesses be responsible and environment-friendly. Studies have shown that 82 per cent of the developed world is willing to pay a premium of up to 20 per cent for products which are considered socially responsible.

Third is the emergence of resource constraints. A growing population and consumption will almost certainly create tremendous pressures on existing raw material, including iron ore, coal, fuels, minerals and even fresh water. Hence, new materials, such as carbon fibres, advanced ceramics, high-temperature semiconductors and bio-based plastics will create breakthroughs in the next one decade. Industries need to be ready to face such transformational times and also manage price volatilities, which we are already facing in terms of almost all raw materials.

Let me now talk of another issue societies are facing—developing sustainable systems.

Towards a global sustainable system

Friends, today, more than 800 million people in India, and about three billion people in the world as a whole, are living in villages, and hence any mission towards global prosperity and happiness has to be inclusive of the rural regions. When you graduate from this campus today, as managers, you have to ensure that the application of enterprise and management systems reaches the most underprivileged population. Some of you may choose to pursue careers along this line and, with your innovation, bring about unforeseen enhancement to the current state. Hence, let us discuss how the sustainable development of 600,000 villages can be achieved through PURA—providing urban amenities in rural areas.

In the past, the government and the private and public sectors have been taking up rural development in parts. For example, starting an educational institution, starting healthcare centres, laying roads, building houses, building a marketing complex, giving a communication link in a particular rural area—these have been taken up in the past as individual activities. During the last few decades, it is our experience that these initiatives start well, just like heavy rain resulting into multiple streams of water flow. A few days after the rain stops, however, all the streams dry up because there are no water bodies to collect the surplus water and store it at the right place. PURA envisages an integrated sustainable development plan with employment generation as the focus, driven by the provisions of the habitat, healthcare, education, skill development, physical and electronic connectivity and marketing as a public–private partnership initiative.

Subsystems of sustainable development

Dear friends, I would first like to discuss what constitutes sustainable development. Sustainable development means integrated thoughts and actions that not only lead to financially robust systems but also keenly focus on societal development, environmental conservation, technological infusion and employment creation. In the context of rural India, it would mean the evolution of socioeconomic entities that transform the means of livelihood and quality of life for 800 million rural citizens with a customized and adaptable action plan that follows the route of citizen empowerment and capacity-building. It could also require the building of a society whose fabric is strongly bounded by a value system of harmony, respect for diversity and care for the environment. Friends, when we discuss today the opportunities and challenges of sustainable development like PURA, we should keep all these aspects in mind.

The mission of PURA, apart from concentrating on reinforcing agriculture, will emphasize on agro-processing, the development of rural craftsmanship, dairy, fish and fish processing, and silk production so that the non-farm revenue for the rural sector is enhanced, based on the core competencies of the region. Let me discuss briefly the components of typical PURA and the method of integration.

PURA: Connectivities which lead to it

PURA essentially requires four levels of connectivity which have to be customized according to local competencies and needs:

- The villages must be connected within themselves and with main towns and metros through good roads and, wherever needed, by railway lines. They must have other infrastructure, such as schools, colleges, hospitals and amenities, for the local population and visitors. This is physical connectivity.
- In the emerging knowledge era, the native knowledge has to be preserved and enhanced with the latest tools of technology, training and research. The villages have to have access to good education from the best teachers wherever they are, must have the benefit of good medical treatment and must have the latest information on their pursuits, including agriculture, fishery, horticulture and food processing. That means they have to have electronic connectivity.
- Once physical and electronic connectivity are enabled, knowledge connectivity is enabled. This can facilitate the ability to increase productivity, the utilization of spare time, awareness of health welfare, ensuring a

market for products, increasing quality conscience, interacting with partners, getting the best equipment, increasing transparency and so, in general, knowledge connectivity that progresses the core competence of the rural environment with additional attention to technology. Hence, these three connectivities in an integrated way lead to economic connectivity.

- Once the three connectivities, namely, physical, electronic and knowledge connectivity, are ensured, they facilitate earning capacity, leading to economic connectivity. When we provide urban amenities to rural areas, it can lead to the upliftment of rural areas, and we çan attract investors, introduce effectively useful systems like rural BPOs and micro- and small-scale industries.

The number of PURA initiatives for the whole country is estimated to be 7000, covering 600,000 villages where 800 million people live. There are a number of operational PURA initiatives in our country started by many educational institutions, healthcare institutions, and industry and other institutions. The Government of India is already moving ahead with the implementation of PURA on the national scale across several districts.

Typical working PURA initiatives

It is possible to get an insight into PURA by studying a few of the operational PURA initiatives that are functioning in different parts of the country—the Periyar PURA, Loni

PURA, Chitrakoot PURA, Meenakshi PURA and Warana PURA. Let me highlight few aspects of the Warana PURA.

Warana PURA: Farmer cooperative in action

Friends, in March 2010, I was in the Warana valley of Kolhapur district. The Warana PURA mission began as a sugar cooperative movement, the vision of a great social leader called Sah-kaar-shri Tatyasaheb Kore, in the 1950s to transform the Warana region, which was a backward area infested with unlawful activities.

The Warana PURA has since then evolved on a cooperative framework and implemented sustainable models based on the core competencies of rural areas covering sixty-nine villages and about four lakh people. This PURA model, which has more than 60,000 farmers, women entrepreneurs and villagers as members, has been giving a consistent dividend of over 250 per cent. The Warana PURA programme has succeeded in creating income generation through value addition to sugar and dairy products, innovative agricultural practices and entrepreneurship, striving towards literacy and healthcare for all. For the welfare of landless villagers, Tatyasaheb Kore envisioned and pioneered the creation of the Warana Poultry and Warana Cooperative Dairy with more than 16,000 milk producers spread over sixty villages.

Similarly, the Warana PURA has also initiated cooperative educational institutions, retail outlets and hospitals for better standards of living. The Warana PURA is an example of how integrated development can be achieved through a tightly knit cooperative structure with value addition and economic empowerment.

Friends, I have specifically explained how integrated rural development can take place through the creation of PURA complexes covering groups of villages in any region. I suggest the creation of a TAPMI PURA for twenty to thirty villages with a population of over 20,000. This type of societal mission will make a greater impact on the society and a large number of rural citizens will be empowered through education, healthcare and employment-generation schemes. These PURA complexes will also give hands-on experience to students and faculty members of TAPMI in system design, system integration and system management, and some of them can certainly take up PURA entrepreneurial missions after graduation.

Economic development, competitiveness and creative leadership

Since I am in the midst of management students, let me discuss the linkage between national economic development and creative leadership.

- A nation's economic development is powered by competitiveness.
- Competitiveness is powered by knowledge power.
- Knowledge power is powered by technology and innovation.
- Technology and innovation are powered by resource investment.
- Resource investment is powered by returns on investment.
- Return on investment is powered by revenue.

- Revenue is powered by volume and repeat sales.
- Volume and repeat sales are powered by customer loyalty.
- Customer loyalty is powered by the quality and value of products.
- The quality and value of products are powered by employee productivity and innovation.
- Employee productivity is powered by employee loyalty.
- Employee loyalty is powered by employee satisfaction.
- Employee satisfaction is powered by the working environment.
- The working environment is powered by management innovation.
- Management innovation is powered by creative leadership.

For success in all the missions, it is essential to have creative leaders. Creative leadership means exercising the vision to change the traditional role from the commander to the coach, manager to mentor, from director to delegator and from one who demands respect to one who facilitates self-respect. For dynamic economic growth with sustainability, we need a large number of creative leaders.

Conclusion: What I will be remembered for?

Finally, I would like to ask you this: what would you like to be remembered for? You have to evolve yourself and shape your life. You should write it on a page. That page may be a very important page in the book of human history. And you will be remembered for creating that one page in the history of the nation—whether that page is a page of invention, a page of innovation, a page of discovery, a page of creating societal change, a page of removing poverty or a page of fighting injustice or planning and executing an energy independence mission for the nation.

I am sure you would like to do something different—out-of-the-box missions, but what are they?

- Will you be remembered for a visionary action for the nation, like Professor Vikram Sarabhai or Jamsetji Tata?
- Will you be remembered for creating a company which finds a place in the top 100 of the Fortune 500 companies from India?
- Will you be remembered for facilitating the creation of fifty PURA initiatives in your region?
- Will you be remembered for becoming the pioneer in developing a smart waterway in the states and interlinking of rivers in the nation?
- Will you be remembered for revitalizing or revolutionizing the integrated primary healthcare centre in a public–private participation model?
- Will you be remembered for working and creating a validated system for the production of 340 million tons of food grains and value addition through food processing by the year 2020?
- Will you be remembered for the modernization of ten million small and medium enterprises (SMEs) and

the addition of another million by providing private-equity funding?

- Will you be remembered as a venture-capital banker by introducing the unique private-equity funding for ideas that will bring new dimensions to society.
- Will you be remembered for bringing about energy independence for the nation?
- Will you be remembered for the action-oriented 'clean home, clean environment, clean state and clean nation'?
- Will you be remembered for developing one million enlightened youths in your region who will participate in the accelerated societal transformation of the nation?

Once again, let me congratulate all the graduating students of the T.A. Pai Institute of Management, Manipal.

My greetings and best wishes to all of you for success in your life.

May God bless you.

Roopa Kudva

Roopa Kudva is the managing director and chief executive officer of Credit Rating Information Services of India Ltd. CRISIL, a subsidiary of Standard & Poor's, is a global analytical company providing ratings, research and risk and policy advisory services. CRISIL is India's leading ratings agency and is also the foremost provider of high-end research and analytics services to the world's largest banks and leading corporations. It delivers analysis, opinions and solutions that make markets function better.

Ms Kudva has led CRISIL's evolution from a leading Indian rating agency to a diversified analytical company with clients ranging from the largest investment banks of the world to tens of thousands of small firms spread across India. Under her leadership, CRISIL's market capitalization has grown four-fold, from Rs 2900 crores to Rs 14,000 crores, and revenues have tripled. Within India, its reach has expanded from nine Indian cities to 150, while, globally, CRISIL's research centres have now expanded to Argentina, China and Poland. During her tenure, CRISIL has pioneered several innovations including rating of mid-sized and small Indian companies and the launch of a unique financial inclusion index for India. She also spearheaded CRISIL's entry into proprietary research outside India by acquiring the UK-based Coalition Development Ltd in 2012.

Earlier, Ms Kudva led CRISIL's ratings business, and also led CRISIL's foray into global research and analytics. Roopa joined CRISIL in 1992, and has more than two decades of global experience across sectors in India, Middle East, Eastern Europe and Mediterranean countries, including a secondment to Standard & Poor's, Paris, as director, financial institutions ratings. In April 2015, after a twenty-two-year innings, Roopa moved on from CRISIL to take up a new assignment as an Omidyar Network (ON) partner and managing director of Omidyar Network India Advisors. Established by Ebay founder Pierre Omidyar, ON is a philanthropic investment firm dedicated to harnessing the power of markets to create an opportunity for people to improve their lives.

Ms Kudva regularly features in lists of the most powerful women in business compiled by prominent publications, including *Fortune* and *Business Today*, and she is a recipient of several prestigious awards including the Outstanding Woman Business Leader of the Year at CNBC TV18's India Business Leader Awards 2012, *India Today*'s Corporate Woman Award 2014 and the Indian Merchants' Chamber's Ladies' Wing's Woman of the Year award 2013–14.

Ms Kudva is an independent director on the board of Infosys Ltd, as well a member of several policy-level committees relating to the Indian financial system, including committees of the Securities and Exchange Board of India (SEBI) and the RBI. She is a member of the External Advisory Committee for evaluating applicants for Payment Bank licences by the RBI. She has also been a member of the executive council of the National Association of Software and Services Companies (NASSCOM). She is a regular speaker at global conferences and seminars by multilateral agencies, market participants and leading academic institutions.

Ms Kudva holds a postgraduate diploma in management from the Indian Institute of Management Ahmedabad and also received the Distinguished Alumnus Award from her alma mater.

Roopa Kudva

Dr Sesha Iyer, director, Professor Abbas Ali Gabula, deputy director, professors on the dais, graduating students, ladies and gentlemen.

Thank you for inviting me to the S.P. Jain Institute of Management and Research. It is an honour and pleasure to be here. The students of the graduating class of today represent some of the brightest and best of the young generation of this nation. You are smart and ambitious, and you have undoubtedly given great thought to your careers. I am not sure what I can talk about that you haven't heard before. So, what I thought I would do is share with you some perspectives derived from my own experience, and I hope you will find that useful.

Most of us are deeply shaped by the experiences of our very young days. I grew up in the 1970s and early 1980s in Assam and received all my pre-MBA education there. It was a gentle and slow existence, surrounded by nature. It was a

---

Convocation address delivered by Ms Roopa Kudva, managing director and chief executive officer of CRISIL, at the S.P. Jain Institute of Management and Research on 26 April 2014. Reproduced with the permission of the author.

world caught in a time warp—by today's standards, there was 'nothing to do'. The way one spent a weekend or holiday was that you got up in the morning, ate your breakfast and ran into the forest nearby to play and returned whenever you were hungry. And there was no one really worrying about where you were, or what you were doing!

I graduated in statistics, and towards the end of my college years, I too faced the question, 'What next?'

I appeared for the CAT. I did so only because a cousin pointed out what she called the best college in India—which in this forum I will refer to only as a certain well-known institute of management in western India, or WIMWI. She told me that once I got there, I would have a lot of options thereafter. So I landed up in Ahmedabad, with no exposure at all to the world of business. I hadn't even heard of Hindustan Lever (now Hindustan Unilever) and when I heard it being mentioned in my first week at business school, I had no idea what it was. A kind classmate told me that this is the company that made Lux soap and Dalda—which, thankfully, I had heard about. So how did business school help me? What did I learn there?

The most important thing I learnt was structured thinking. This is about approaching a problem by beginning with the first principles. I have found this extremely useful over the years and never more so than today when, as the CEO of a company, I have to process a variety of information, views and analyses. I find that starting from first principles and asking the very basic questions always helps me identify key issues and take a holistic approach. It also helps in keeping things simple.

The second thing I found very valuable about my business school education was the exposure to, and learning from, an outstanding student body. Not only were the students very bright, but many were highly accomplished in so many spheres like dramatics, sports and music. Initially, this was daunting—I found the academics very difficult, and had to get used to the fact that I would be nowhere near the top of the class. But, looking back, I can tell you that a lot of my great learnings at business school didn't come from the classroom, but from my peers. I think being surrounded by people who are better and brighter than you are helps you raise your game. It also helps you understand what your own unique strengths are. Years later, in CRISIL, too, I never really was the best analyst. The trick to good leadership is in recognizing the merit in others and harnessing it. Today, too, I am surrounded by people brighter than I am. How I make a difference is by bringing in my unique strengths. And I will come back to this theme later.

As you enter the workforce today, what will be your approach? What will drive you? How will you measure your success? As you chase your ambitions and look to get ahead, it helps to remember that you are a part of the privileged few in India. I am always overwhelmed by the fact that people like me who entered the workforce in the late 1980s and early 1990s benefited significantly from the huge uplift that the Indian economy saw after the reforms and liberalization. No generation before us had seen the trajectory of growth that we saw. And I can never forget that this country also gave me the opportunity to benefit from a quality education at practically no cost. I believe it behoves me, therefore, to make all that count for something. And this belief has shaped my attitude to my work and career. People talk of 'giving back' to mean giving to charity and doing something at some point in the social sector. I think those are indeed extremely important things. But you can do much to give back through your core job too—by the impact you create with your work, by taking responsible business decisions, by keeping the purpose of your business more important than making money, by using your business role to create opportunities for small businesses, by creating opportunities for people from not-so-privileged backgrounds and by ensuring your organization creates value for all stakeholders. If a sense of giving back and a commitment to a greater good is what drives you in your day-to-day work in the corporate world, you will more often than not see career success too. It is a different approach to take than focusing on pay, promotion and climbing up the ladder. But I believe it is far more rewarding. You, too, are a privileged group of people. And I would urge you, do make that count for something.

The fact that you made it to a leading school means that you value excellence. However, something that is not adequately appreciated is that excellence is a long-term journey. In this age of instant fixes, this fact is very, very important to recognize, because it will define your working life. I have held just two jobs in the last twenty-eight years—this will surely seem very odd to you, but it worked for me. Several people come up to me and say—after a couple of years of working in one sector or industry—that they have learnt everything and want to move on. Sometimes they say this even in six months. Now this is just not possible, because excellence is the outcome of doing something repeatedly for many, many years, again and again and when you are ready to give up, doing it yet again. As Hesiod, the Greek poet of the eighth century BCE, said, 'Before the gates of excellence, the high gods have placed sweat; long is the road thereto and rough and steep at first; but when the heights are reached, then there is ease, though grievously hard in the winning.' The fact is that there are no shortcuts, no quick fixes. And there is a certain relentlessness of repetition and focus on minutiae associated with the pursuit of excellence—witness the tens of thousands of hours sportsmen and musicians spend on perfecting their craft—and that, too, may not be enough to get them to the very top. The enemy of excellence is saying 'I get bored quickly.'

I would also like to emphasize communication skills. Never have communication skills been more important than they are today. Companies are global, and the ability to communicate and connect with people across the world is a key trait for career success. At CRISIL, we have a younger workforce—people like yourselves—that demands more frequent feedback, wants to know the bigger picture and the strategy of the company much more than what we did when I was in the initial stages of my career.

Therefore, it's important for leaders of today to communicate well and communicate frequently. Most of us are not naturally good communicators—you have to work at it. When you come from a small town—like I did—there is a tendency to presume people in the cities are more accomplished because they have had broader exposure, can communicate better and their awareness levels are more acute. So I learnt to speak well. In those days, there was very little television, so I used to spend a lot of time listening to BBC Radio, which helped to improve my diction. I also enthusiastically participated in college debates, which increased my confidence and knowledge base.

You live in a highly competitive world. But I will still say this to you—don't obsess about how you are doing. If you are relaxed and enjoy your work, you have a better chance of being successful. By that I mean, take your work very, very seriously, but don't take yourself too seriously. While healthy ambition is a good thing, don't obsessively compare yourself with others on every small thing. If you acknowledge the fact that in a working life of thirty-five or more years, it is natural that you will have several setbacks and years when things don't go so well, it will help you a great deal. Recognize that it is okay. In the long run, if you do the right things, generally the right things happen for you. And do make mistakes, but more importantly, don't repeat them. Also, expect your plan to come up short more often than you want it to. The first time I got admission to the WIMWI, I was not allowed to join because Assam was then in the throes of an anti-foreigner agitation and I could not complete my final exams on time. I had to reappear for CAT the next year. I spent the intervening period, among other things, teaching kindergarten students because I didn't have a back-up plan. I was lucky that it was great fun, but that may not always be the case!

And finally, get ahead on the basis of what you are good at. In other words, play to your strengths. For this, you need to make an honest assessment of what you are not good at, and this is never easy to do. But do revel in what makes you different in a positive way instead of focusing too much on your shortcomings. Organizations look for a diversity of skills and competencies and not for people who are clones. And while most organizations will have two or three key skills or capabilities that dominate, you will notice that people at the top may not necessarily be the best on that score. So it is not the person with the best engineering skills that makes it to the top of an engineering company, but the person will have other key strengths that make them stand out and rise to the top. Let me give you some examples: Louis V. Gerstner Jr, the legendary CEO of IBM between 1993 and 2002, previously worked at RJR Nabisco, American Express and McKinsey—none of which were in information technology or hardware. Richard Branson has dyslexia, but still runs so many businesses successfully. My favourite example is of Katharine Graham, who was born into a privileged family, but was never brought up to run a business. A family tragedy pitched her to the helm of the Washington Post Company, and she led the newspaper through some of its biggest successes—including breaking the Watergate scandal that eventually resulted in the resignation of the then US president, Richard Nixon. And she made the *Washington Post* into a huge financial success. When the newspaper went public in 1971, the share price was $6.50. When she stepped down in 1991, it was $221. And this was a woman who for many years had a piece of paper under the glass on her table that said, 'Liabilities to the left, assets to the right'!

So, work hard and do good; but don't forget to enjoy the journey. I wish you great success.

Ranjana Kumar

Ms Ranjana Kumar is a prominent Indian banker with varied experience of around forty-four years. Ms Kumar holds a Bachelor of Arts degree, and is a gold medallist.

Ms Kumar retired as a vigilance commissioner from the Central Vigilance Commission and has held several significant positions in her career, including that as the chairperson and managing director of the Indian Bank, chairperson of the National Bank for Agriculture and Rural Development (NABARD), executive director holding concurrent charge as chairman and managing director of the Canara Bank, and CEO of the US operations of Bank of India based in New York.

Under her chairmanship, Ms Kumar was instrumental in restructuring and turning around the Indian Bank, then the weakest public sector undertaking (PSU) bank, from a loss making entity, into a profitable bank.

Ms Kumar took over the 'weak' US operations of the Bank of India as chief executive officer, US operations, at New York, 1995–99 and ensured that suitable systems and policies were put in place. The bank was awarded a 'strong' rating by the US Federal Reserve in 1998.

She has been recipient of the Best Woman Director 2014 by the Asian Centre for Corporate Governance and Sustainability, the Lifetime Achievement Award in the Banking Industry (including PSU Banks and Private Sector Banks and the Reserve Bank of India) for the year 2012 by *Businessworld* special issue, BMA (Bombay Management Association), Woman Achiever of the Year Award 2008–09 and Banker of the Year 2002 Award by *Business Standard*, among others.

Ms Ranjana Kumar has authored a book titled *A New Beginning: The Turnaround Story of Indian Bank.*

Ms Kumar regularly addresses top managements of a cross-section of PSUs, important academic institutions including IIMs and IITs on various aspects concerning management, leadership and issues relating to human resource management both in India and abroad.

She has been appointed by the Reserve Bank of India and Central Vigilance Commission, as chairperson of the Advisory Board on Bank, Commercial and Financial Frauds (ABBCFF).

Ranjana Kumar

It is indeed a privilege for me to be here on this very august occasion of the sixteenth annual convocation at IIM Kozhikode, a great academic institution of our country. This is indeed a moment of pride for not only the students, but also their parents and faculty who have worked so hard.

I would like to share with you today the learnings from my experience. At the outset, I would like to tell you that you are indeed very fortunate to have been born in this age, not only in terms of massive strides of development taking place the world over and in India, but also in particular the advancement in the field of technology, whereby information and data on any subject is available to you within seconds, enabling you to have a better perspective of issues and matters.

At the same time, the present scenario the world over has become so complex that management has assumed greater significance than ever before. The current era of

---

Convocation address delivered by Ms Ranjana Kumar, chairperson, National Bank for Agriculture and Rural Development, and former chairperson and managing director, Indian Bank, at the Indian Institute of Management Kozhikode on 22 March 2014. Reproduced with the permission of the author.

liberalization, globalization, mergers and acquisitions have made competition very intense, and this intensity would only increase in the times to come, with a surge in the number of players in the market, greater quality consciousness, the stress on margins of profit, the war on pricing, the multiplicity of laws to be complied with, stringent regulations on pollution, fair business practices, a very vibrant media and so on.

Therefore, today's manager, as most of you will be, would require, apart from knowledge of the subject proper and the need to keep it updated, to be a multifaceted personality, with equanimity of mind and lots of common sense and logic, and abundant mental and physical energy.

Here, I would like to list out various traits of a performer. Technically speaking, a performer in an organization is one who achieves the 'budget'. But when we speak of an overall view, a performer is one who has made a difference to the organization.

- One who takes initiative—has a 'never say die' attitude and would like to experiment with different strategies to achieve goals.
- One who is knowledgeable and has an appetite to take measured and manageable risks.
- One who will not only seek clarification on issues, but be a solution-finder (that is what the country needs today).
- One who can deliver in the most trying situations.
- One who will motivate and bring the entire team together by creating a work environment that is objective, fair and transparent—an environment conducive to growth.

Remember, the graph of life never remains static, it keeps moving up and down, whether it be for an individual, an organization or any business set-up. When the graph goes down, people tend to get despondent and discouraged, little realizing that this is the time when they need to look inwards and carry out an objective and detailed analysis of what went wrong and how they would be able to take corrective steps for the future. This is, therefore, a time for fresh learning and also some unlearning of certain beliefs, thought patterns, concepts, behaviours and so on. Experience teaches—and it has been wisely said that when organizations go through difficult times, the halo around them hides their strengths. It is these strengths which they would need to capitalize on and further cultivate in order to restructure the organization.

In the process of restructuring, the qualities of resilience, tenacity, willpower and greater self-confidence are built among the workforce.

On the other hand, when the organizations are performing well, the halo around them hides their weaknesses. It is therefore prudent, and in their own interest at this time, for such organizations to ensure a critical analysis and close monitoring of performance, so as not to become complacent and overconfident. This would ensure that such organizations do not face shocks and surprises.

It is important to be able to identify and seize opportunities when they arise. For this, you need to be not only knowledgeable, but also aware of the developments taking place around you and in the industry. It is important to believe that you have adequate untapped potential which you will be able to realize only upon taking up challenges.

However, many a time it has been seen that we miss out on great opportunities, unwilling or hesitant to put our potential to test. The Greeks say that the goddess of opportunity has hair in front but is bald behind, and therefore, you have to seize her (opportunity) upfront because she will turn around very quickly and you will be left stroking a bald head. Many also say some people are 'just lucky'. So what is the definition of luck? The answer is 'when preparedness on your part meets opportunity; that is luck'.

It is very important to know the strengths of our team, and to be able to utilize people as per their strengths. This has been a relatively new concept in management, coming out of an observation that, many a time, while we are able to identify the task to be done, it takes a much longer time to decide who should be doing it. It has also been said that in organizations, a larger percentage of people take work as routine as they are not given an opportunity to 'play to their strengths'. Jack Welch, chief of General Electric, said, 'When you place people as per their strengths and give them wings, you don't really have to manage them.' This means that people's performance need not be monitored when they are entrusted with assignments in tune with their strengths.

We should recognize the importance of delegation and empowerment. Delegation should not be misconstrued as 'handing over control', for the overall responsibility will always with the delegator. The experience of many world-class organizations indicates that empowering is one of the best ways to make people involved and committed in organizational efforts. Excellent organizations are those that empower their employees for their own growth as well as for enhancing organizational performance. It is believed that employees' creative ability and development are realized through empowerment.

When people are empowered, they will take decisions. When they take decisions, there will be mistakes. The DNA of the organization should not be such that there is a knee-jerk reaction or a panic button pressed when mistakes occur. In fact, what needs to be addressed under such circumstances is not 'who is responsible for the mistake' but 'how did the mistake occur', and what steps need to be taken to ensure that it does not reoccur. This would also ensure that employee morale is not adversely affected.

We should remember that effective communication is one of the pillars of the success of an organization, and therefore, we must be very careful while giving instructions—clarity in communication—and also be careful while receiving instructions. In fact, in case of the slightest doubt, we should re-confirm that the recipient has clearly understood what we have communicated. Similarly, we must ensure that our understanding of the instructions is in conformity with the instructions given to us. It was Peter Drucker, the well-known management guru, who said that 'around 95 per cent of problems in organizations occur because of a breakdown in communication, and only around 5 per cent happen because of technical reasons'.

One important piece of advice I would like to share with you is the need to check your thoughts regularly, at least twice in a day. It is very essential for us to ensure that we remove the unproductive and wasteful thoughts that come into our mind from time to time. This should be cultivated as a habit, as it has several benefits, such as abundant energy levels, greater clarity while taking decisions, greater focus on issues, and above all, a healthy mind. Therefore, whenever negative thoughts come to our mind, we should cultivate an immediate response of 'pressing the delete button', as it were. Mark Twain, the renowned American author, was quoted saying, 'A lot of things I worried about in life never really happened.'

We should try to get over the habit of criticizing others as this creates negative vibes for us and not for the other person. Learn to accept people as they are, get along with them and learn to work with them. Do not try to change people. At the most, you can inspire them with your own conduct and behaviour.

It is advisable to cultivate good friends. At least one or two who know you really well, who understand you, with whom you can open up and share any problem or any issue which is bothering you, and who will hear you out patiently. Being able to speak your mind in difficult times serves as a tremendous relief, making you feel light even though the issue in question may not have been entirely resolved.

Also try to cultivate good hobbies. Be it music of any kind, gardening, any kind of outdoor sports and so on, and you will experience creativity through them; they also serve as great stress busters.

We must learn to accept life as it unfolds before us. It is, therefore, important to keep our levels of enthusiasm and optimism at a high, notwithstanding the circumstances. Whereas it is an accepted belief that hard work, sincerity and commitment will ensure success, it may not happen all the time as life tends to be uncertain. In fact, people of experience and wisdom have said, 'The best part of about life is its uncertainty', and hence, we should never lose faith in our own acumen, our potential, keeping in mind that patience is also a virtue, and take everything in our stride.

In conclusion, I would like to say that as Indians, by and large, we are not aggressive people. But we must cultivate the quality of assertiveness as a positive quality in our beliefs, in our values, in our understanding and never agree to do something which would make us feel uncomfortable at a later date. Ethics and integrity at all times are very valuable assets, ones we should never compromise upon, notwithstanding the circumstances. In recent times, we have seen many great individuals and also companies the world over, and in our own country, who enjoyed powerful reputations, falling from grace overnight for reasons better known to them, be it over-ambition, greed or any kind of indiscretion. There are important lessons for all of us to learn from such cases.

It is not my intention to be philosophic; however, our *sanskar*, or culture, tells us that while as mortals, we take many births, the soul is constant and is what embodies our basic nature. The major qualities of the soul are calmness, peacefulness, happiness, strength, love and purity—all positive qualities. I would like to repeat, these are the qualities of our basic/original nature. Please note that anger, jealousy, hatred and arrogance (*ahankar*) do not figure in this list and, therefore, have to be consciously avoided. For, with these negative traits, we would never be able to create a healthy environment, conducive to growth, at our workplace or at home.

I would like to congratulate each one of you who is graduating today.

You will now be entering a very exciting phase in your life. Remember, after college, experience will be your most valuable teacher. Therefore, be open to learning the new as well as being open to unlearning certain perspectives and habits, when this change makes sense.

I wish you all a very meaningful and fulfilling career and life ahead.

God bless you.

Anand Mahindra

Anand Mahindra is chairman and managing director of Mahindra & Mahindra Ltd. He graduated with honours (magna cum laude) from Harvard College and received an MBA from the Harvard Business School.

Following a number of leadership positions within the Mahindra Group, he was appointed chairman and managing director in 2012. He is the co-founder of the Harvard Business School Association of India and a co-promoter of Kotak Mahindra Finance Ltd, which in 2003 was converted into a bank. He currently serves as the honorary ambassador of Foreign Investment Promotion for the Republic of Korea, a member of the International Advisory Council of Singapore's Economic Development Board, a member of the Harvard Global Advisory Council and a member of the global board of advisors of the Council of Foreign Relations, New York.

Anand Mahindra is included in *Fortune* magazine's list of the world's fifty greatest leaders in 2014. *Fortune* magazine also named him as one of the top twenty-five most powerful business people in Asia for the year 2011.

His recent awards include the Global Leadership Award from the US–India Business Council, the Business Courage Award 2012 from the Asia Business Leadership Forum, Business Leader of the Year 2012 from NDTV, and the *Forbes India* Leadership Awards 2013 'Entrepreneur of the Year'. He is the first Indian recipient of the Harvard Medal 2014 by the Harvard Alumni Association given for extraordinary service to Harvard University.

Anand Mahindra

The graduating class of 2014 and their families, Mr A.M. Naik, chairman, board of governors, members of the faculty, ladies and gentlemen.

It is almost customary for convocation speakers to terrify their audience by telling them that they are about to begin their lives. If I used that cliché with you, it would sound patently unfair, wouldn't it? I would imagine that all of you probably feel as if a good portion of your life has already been well earned and well spent!

The very fact that you were admitted to IIM Ahmedabad means that you have been running the race of life for quite a while now. You probably studied diligently throughout school, worked even harder in college, engaged in a diverse set of extracurricular pursuits, worked strenuously to achieve high scores in the entrance tests, and finally, adopted a back-breaking pace just to make it through the last two years and qualify to wear those robes. The world lies at your feet today.

Convocation address delivered by Mr Anand Mahindra, chairman and managing director of the Mahindra Group, at the Indian Institute of Management Ahmedabad on 22 March 2014. Reproduced with the permission of the author.

So let me confirm that you are not fledgling, inexperienced birds about to fly out of the nest and you need not be intimidated by this supposedly imminent and momentous commencement of your lives.

There is, however, a very different danger you face. The danger that forty years from now, you will be reflecting upon your life and declaring to your friends that your days at IIM Ahmedabad were the best days of your life.

Now I am not refuting or challenging the fact that you might have thoroughly enjoyed your stint here. What I wish for you is that things only get better from here onwards. And I want you to hit the ground running and have as few wasted moments as is humanly possible.

I have found that the days that I see now as the wasted days of my life were those when I didn't take an acceptable risk that I could have conceivably taken, when I didn't ask myself if there was a new and different way to do what I was doing, when I didn't set my sights as high as I possibly could have.

To give you an example, let me take you back more than two decades ago, when we formed a joint venture (JV) with Ford Motor to make passenger vehicles. Why did we do that? Well, because at that time, we had only just started making vehicles with hard tops, and were diffident about our capability to transition to the modern car-making world. We needed a mother ship in case our little spacecraft didn't survive out there. Some years later, during the tenure of that JV, when our home-grown Mahindra engineers came up with the concept of the Scorpio SUV, we dutifully sought our JV partner's advice and assistance. I will never forget the day we displayed the model of the Scorpio to the top brass at Ford, who had gathered at the tiny facility of a boutique engineering firm in the UK.

We showed them a crude clay model of the Scorpio and shared our development budget with them. They seemed impressed and, right away, the vice chairman of the company offered to depute a team of seasoned Ford engineers to assist us in the development of the vehicle. At that point, the chairman interjected and said, 'No, let's not send any engineers at all. If we do, this vehicle may come out looking like a Ford car, and costing just as much. If these guys can really develop this car they've just shown us at the cost they claim they can, then I think we are the ones who should be learning from them.'

I owe Ford a debt of gratitude for leaving us to fend for ourselves. Because when I look back upon these events, I know that the choice Ford made put us solidly on the path of self-reliance. But I admit that I have often wondered how things would have turned out had Ford made a different choice.

What if they had not abandoned us to do the Scorpio alone? It is obvious that we would not have built the capabilities we possess today.

So I have asked myself: why did I make that offer in the first place? What was the source of diffidence that made us ask for an alliance? Could we have been more audacious, and attempted the impossible right from the start? Why did it take such an enormous leap of faith for us to conceive our own indigenously designed vehicle? Why did it take so long to believe in ourselves?

The conclusion I arrived at was that embedded in my generation's psyche was a fear of flying, a deep fear of failure, a character trait that is the mortal enemy of entrepreneurship.

And even when we indulged in entrepreneurship, we tended to stay within our comfort zones. An example of this that I enjoy citing is that of a good friend of mine, an outstanding businessman who has grown his family business into a formidable footwear chain throughout India. One of the extensions to his business was a new high-quality brand, conceived and created for a more upscale segment—a brand called Mochi.

It has performed extremely well here in India, but I recall a conversation with him, in which I asked him why he hadn't ventured abroad with that product, even as new and differentiated footwear brands were sprouting in the Western world. I told him that I could easily envision Mochi selling on a high street in London. It didn't seem too outlandish an idea; frankly, Mochi even sounded like a long-lost relative of Gucci! He was honest enough to admit to me that he just wasn't ready to take that risk; he was doing fine in India and the pond here was large enough.

I began pondering on why we were so timid, why we were afraid to compete in the toughest arenas. Why did some American college kids from my generation believe they could take on global heavyweights from out of their dorm rooms, while we believed we first needed to compete in the flyweight class?

Well, I put myself on the couch, so to speak, and subjected myself to some amateur psychoanalysis, and I want to share one hypothesis that I came up with. It's a narrative I've shared before in other gatherings, and if any of you have heard it before, please accept my apologies. However, I never tire of retelling it.

It goes back to my high school days at a boarding school in the hill station of Ooty. The year was 1970 and my class was giving its final exam for the Indian Schools Certificate. The exam was conducted in a large auditorium, with a stage upon which a large iron safe was placed. Just before the exam commenced, the headmaster, wearing black academic robes, looking like a character out of a Harry Potter movie, walked ceremoniously to the safe, opened it with the combination code in his possession, and extracted from it the question papers for that subject which had been dispatched to India from the UK! Those papers were then distributed to the students, along with blue books, and once our time was up, our blue answer books were collected and put into the safe, from where they were dispatched back to the UK for correction! And this process applied to every subject taught to us except Indian languages. Now I want you to imagine what subconscious messages were being transmitted to our young minds. The message was that even twenty-five years after Independence, we Indians were not competent enough to correct our own examination papers, let alone set them. What subliminal effect do you think it would have had on me and my classmates? Could one have invented any better way to subtly discourage a group of young people from believing they could take on the mighty West?

I believe that this psychological legacy of colonialism was at least as pernicious as the memories of physical humiliation. Why on earth did we allow this residue to remain for so long? We were in a state of mind best summed up by this Urdu *sher*:

Ajab ye zindagi ki
Kaid hai har insaan

Rihayi maangta hai aur
Riha hone se darta hai.

It essentially means that even though we long for our freedom, we are mortally afraid of being released.

But I must also tell you the amusing and gratifying sequel to this narrative. I first told this story at a gathering of Indians in Silicon Valley over ten years ago. Some months after that event, I received a mail from one of the members of the audience, who said he couldn't resist sending me a copy of a news item he had read in a British newspaper. It seems that one of the three main UK examination boards—the AQA—had reached an understanding with a private company in India to outsource the marking of 500,000 examination papers. The papers would be digitized and sent to India for marking and returned to the UK! I guess life does come full circle and some larger force up there possesses an ironic sense of humour!

Now I won't blame you if your reaction is that this story is simply an entertaining excuse, a personal rationalization for the timidity of my generation. Be that as it may, my submission to you is that your generation has no such excuses.

You all were schooled at a time when no subliminal signals of inferiority were sent out to you. On the contrary, you have been students during an era when India's star was on the ascendant. You grew up and studied at a time when the world's gaze was on India, and investors began flocking to it. A time when the world believed that India was pregnant with the potential to become an economic superpower. (It's another matter, of course, that we risk entering the Guinness book of records for the world's lengthiest pregnancy!)

There is nothing, therefore, that prevents all of you from aspiring, from the very start, to be world-beaters in all you do. You can dare to be different, dare to disturb the universe. You carry no mental shackles that impede you from creating businesses that will command the attention of the globe. Your objective must be to conquer the world, not just your neighbourhood.

At this point I would like to admit that I have an ulterior motive for sharing these stories, a not-so-hidden agenda. And that is to make you seize a future that is staring you in the face. I truly believe we are at the threshold of an age of entrepreneurship in India. And no, this is not something that will suffer a marathon pregnancy. My evidence is admittedly anecdotal, but I see clear signposts to a visible future.

Over the past two decades, since liberalization, a number of trends have begun converging and leading to a critical mass of the elements needed for a breakout of entrepreneurship.

First, of course, is the dramatic rise in the number of young people who have earned a good technical or business education.

Second is the phenomenal rise in the value of our market capitalization, which provides the incentive to these young people to stay on in India and look for a pay-off right here at home. Since 2007, Indians have founded 8 per cent of all technology and engineering start-ups in the US, and 14 per cent of all Silicon Valley companies. Obviously, we have entrepreneurship in our DNA. It's time to bring the show back home.

The third is the much-awaited sprouting of venture capital (VC) firms and networks, which provide the necessary fuel for start-ups. Despite problems of exit, PE (private equity) and VC investments grew by 46 per cent in the first half of fiscal 2014, and organizations like the Indian Angel Network are growing like a virus. The Indian government only last week announced its plans to set up a $1 billion venture fund that would be seeded by Silicon Valley heroes of ethnic Indian origin.

Finally, and most important, is the role of new technologies in generating a multiplicity of options for new business models.

Information technology spawned a generation of Indian businesses in the outsourcing arena during the 1990s. But the Internet and smart connectivity are generating new ventures to a degree that will dwarf that outsourcing boom. Internet penetration is finally gathering steam, and new and cheap smartphones will dramatically deepen that penetration.

In this arena, Indian start-ups don't suffer the disadvantages of the old generation of entrepreneurs, for whom poor infrastructure was a major impediment.

Technology allows us to trump infrastructure. In fact, the lack of physical infrastructure itself provides entrepreneurial opportunities to provide virtual infrastructure. For example, impossible traffic conditions and congested cities will accelerate e-commerce in India. And poor recreational facilities only mean that our dependence on 4G-enabled entertainment in the palm of our hand will explode.

Unlike some of the closely held industrial technologies of the past, today's technology already resides in India, and there is nothing to prevent a tiny team, say, in Bengaluru, from making the world its market.

It's no surprise then that Facebook recently bought a small start-up called Little Eye Labs in Bengaluru, giving them an early pay-off to their perspiration. This is just the beginning of a tidal wave of such buyouts, which will only serve to enhance the incentives for risk-takers. Technology is also acting as a wildly disruptive force in shaping industry structure.

Facebook pays $19 billion for WhatsApp, and makes giant telecom firms shiver because of their plan to offer free telephony. Technologies such as 3D printing and embedded intelligence are turbocharging traditional manufacturing and enhancing its competitiveness. Hence, I see no reason why India can't lead the world in 'intelligent' manufacturing, and small factory start-ups could very well challenge the hegemony of older and larger manufacturing companies.

If the old competitive landscape could be compared to a placid river upon which giant barges had right of way, think of this new disruptive and unpredictable competitive environment as white-water rapids, better suited to small and nimble kayaks that can manoeuvre between the shifting currents. Evolution is now favouring the small and the agile, and the old barriers to entry are fast eroding.

I say again, the age of entrepreneurship is upon us, and I urge you to embrace it. Not just because of the economic rewards that lie in store for you, but also because your innovation could provide the much-needed answers to the many problems that still snap at our heels. This country is crying out for better healthcare, education, nutrition, water and sanitation. Your creativity can provide an opportunity for you to do well even as you do good.

This is not to downplay the virtues and the rewards of a more conventional career option. I compliment all of you who have landed plum jobs at blue-chip firms and consultancies and investment banks. In fact, I sincerely hope at least one of you might have chosen my group to work with. But I worry that if a good number of you have not chosen to leverage this age of entrepreneurship, then who will?

If an IIM grad does not showcase the 'next big thing', then who will?

If one of you does not build a New Age company that will command the admiration of the globe, then who will?

Yes, many of you who try to be entrepreneurs will fail. But the failure to try, the failure to take any risk is perhaps the greatest failure of all.

On the other hand, if you learn to celebrate the learnings that come from failure, then I guarantee you that success will eventually come, and that however enjoyable a time you've had in college and here at IIM, your best days will indeed lie ahead of you.

As you continue your journey, one thing you can count on is that the rules of the game are going to change. Make sure you're the one changing them.

Good luck, and Godspeed.

Arun Maira

Any discussion on policy and the future of India is enriched with Arun Maira's views, and not just because he was a member of the Planning Commission of India for five years till June 2014. Arun is one of those rare people who have held leadership positions in both the private as well as the public sector, bringing a unique perspective on how the two can work together to foster growth for India. He has led three rounds of participative and comprehensive scenario-building for the future of India: in 1999 (with the Confederation of Indian Industry), 2005 (with the World Economic Forum) and 2011 (with the Planning Commission).

In his career spanning five decades, Arun has led several organizations, including the Boston Consulting Group in India. In the early part of his career, he spent twenty-five years in the Tata Group at various important positions. He was also a member of the board of Tata Motors (then called TELCO). After leaving the Tatas, Arun joined Arthur D. Little Inc. (ADL), the international management consultancy in the US, where he advised companies across sectors and geographies on their growth strategies and handling transformational change.

Another decade later, Arun was back in India, this time as the chairman of the Boston Consulting Group, a position he held for eight years till 2008. The other leadership positions he has held include being the chairman of the Axis Bank Foundation and Save the Children, India. He was also board member of the India Brand Equity Foundation, the Indian Institute of Corporate Affairs, the UN Global Compact and World Wide Fund for Nature (WWF) India.

Recognizing his astute understanding of both macro as well as micro policy issues, Arun has been involved in several government committees and organizations, including the National Innovation Council. He has been on the board of several companies as well as educational institutions and has chaired several national committees of the Confederation of Indian Industries (CII).

In 2009, Arun was appointed as a member of the Planning Commission, which is led by the prime minister of India. At this minister-level position, he led the development of strategies for the country on issues relating to industrialization and urbanization, and drove the formulation of policies and programmes in these areas. He also advised the Commission on its future role.

With his vast experience and expertise, Arun is indeed a thought leader. He is invited to speak at various forums and has written several books that capture his insights.

His most recent book, published in May 2014, is *Redesigning the Aeroplane while Flying: Reforming Institutions*. His earlier books include *Remaking India: One Country, One Destiny*; *Transforming Capitalism: Improving the World for Everyone*, and *Shaping the Future: Aspirational Leadership in India and Beyond*.

Arun Maira

Salutations.

For the past five years, I have been sitting in India's cockpit, the national Planning Commission, from where I could get a perspective of the changes sweeping through India. Every year, the chief ministers of all Indian states come to the Planning Commission to explain the progress their states are making and the challenges they are facing. The Planning Commission oversees the central government ministries, too, and all sectors of the Indian economy. When the Planning Commission prepared the country's twelfth five-year plan in 2012, it deployed a process for the first time to listen widely to the people of the country. Almost a thousand civil society organizations, representing all sections of Indian society, and dozens of business associations participated in an exercise to gather the views of citizens about what mattered most to them and the opportunities they saw for change in the country.

Convocation address delivered by Mr Arun Maira, management consultant and former member, Planning Commission of India, at the Indian Institute of Management Rohtak on 15 March 2014. Reproduced with the permission of the author.

With these myriad inputs from many perspectives, and using techniques of systems analysis and scenario planning, we were able to see the principal forces that are shaping India. And we could hear the signals beneath the deep rumbling of Indian democracy. The people are yearning for the reform of the country's institutions—the government, political parties and business institutions too. Citizens and businesses want institutions to be more responsive. They want them to deliver results more effectively. They want institutions cleaned up of the rust of corruption that is corroding them.

What will be India's future? Three plausible scenarios were distilled from this intensive exercise. Scenarios are not predictions. They are projections of what is most likely to emerge if certain actions are taken, and if they are not.

I will describe the three scenarios. Then I will explain the actions that must be taken to produce the scenario the citizens want. I will also explain why I am an India optimist.

The first scenario is called 'Muddling Along'.

In the background are pictures of the lives of people. A few have become very wealthy with the opening of the economy in the last twenty years. Like peacocks, they strut around and show off their new wealth. Meanwhile, millions of little birds are scrambling for opportunities to improve their lives. Their sense of inequity in the system is driving people to protest against institutions. Some movements of protest have turned violent. Tigers are growling and wolves prowling. The security of citizens is threatened.

Muddling Along is the scenario of India where the system is crying for reform, and some reforms are initiated. However, these are piecemeal, do not address core governance issues and therefore, are not effective. Centralized government systems struggle with demands for decentralization. Small enterprises are sought to be encouraged, but the agenda of big business dominates. The policy conflict between subsidies and the financial stability of the economy remains unresolved. The economy grows but hardly achieves its full potential—insufficient social and political cohesion remains a threatening source of instability. This increases lack of trust in institutions, resulting in continuing protests and a political logjam.

The second scenario is called 'Falling Apart'.

In a picture of this scenario made by a young girl, the leaders are shown as buffaloes wallowing in a pond. The children outside the pond want clean water, better education and opportunities for decent work when they grow up. But the leaders cannot agree on a solution. When one buffalo has an idea and rises, the others will not move. Then another gets an idea and wants to move, but the first says 'you did not cooperate with me so I will not support you.'

This scenario emerges when India remains stuck in a centralized governance system which tries to exert control, in the face of demands for devolution, with its centralized mega schemes and projects, and by the 'redistribution' of wealth through a system of handouts and subsidies. The impatience and political logjam that result put India under severe stress. In a system where hardly any institutional reforms are made, a vicious cycle emerges which results in the political logjam becoming so severe that the government can barely function. Extremism infects more areas of the country. Stand-offs between central government institutions and between the Centre and the states become rigid. Civil society protest movements take up non-negotiable stances. The political logjam becomes worse.

Governments try to win popularity with increasing handouts. Handouts strain governments' finances. Investments slacken. Employment needs do not grow as rapidly as the workforce, so India's demographic changes become a ticking time bomb. Handouts do not incentivize innovation and entrepreneurship, but instead create dependency. A cash-strapped government is unable to achieve its goal of poverty alleviation through subsidies.

The third scenario is 'The Flotilla Advances'.

India is a land of democracy and enterprise. India progresses when its people are empowered. When like fireflies they rise up, with their own light, they will together change the darkness around themselves to light. Many fireflies are arising in India but their growth is hampered by a governance system that smothers their energies.

India is a flotilla of many independent boats that must move together. We have twenty-eight states and many political parties and private enterprises. India is not a uniform monolith. It is racially, linguistically, religiously and politically the most diverse country in the world. All people must want to go in the same direction, and they must learn to cooperate to proceed.

This third scenario of fireflies arising and the flotilla advancing is the future of India with a federal governance system in which the wheels begin to mesh more smoothly, in which local governance institutions and small enterprises are nurtured and grow effectively.

Responding to the widespread demand for institutional reforms, the government vigorously takes up the necessary reforms in government processes and regulatory systems, along with economic reforms. The central government's financial assistance to the states is altered to give the states more flexibility to devise local solutions. Institutional capacity-building, especially in local governance, is given high priority in the government's rural and urban programmes. People begin to see change on the ground. They are engaged, not alienated.

Each of these three scenarios is a result of the different directions the forces shaping India can take. The Planning Commission gave the three scenarios to the National Council of Applied Economic Research (NCAER) to compute what the GDP growth rate and the rate of reduction of poverty would be in each of them.

The NCAER computed that India's GDP growth will remain stuck at below 5 per cent if we do not get the flotilla to advance. However, if we get the flotilla to advance and enable the fireflies to rise, India's GDP growth will exceed 9 per cent per annum and poverty will reduce much faster.

It is worthwhile to step back in time to 2006, when the World Economic Forum (WEF) had prepared three scenarios of India's future. Then, too, the analysis had shown that the principal forces that would determine India's progress were rising inequalities and the weakness of India's institutions. It is noteworthy that the WEF's scenarios came out very similar to the scenarios prepared by the Planning Commission. The WEF's analysis in 2006 showed that India's GDP would grow to over 9 per cent, as it did, but then would decline to below 6 per cent in six or seven years, as it has, if India's institutions were not fixed in good time. The call to fix the institutions was not heeded. People have been losing faith in the political dispensation. Growth has fallen.

The WEF's scenarios had revealed in 2006 what the Planning Commission's scenario analysis reaffirmed in 2012. India must reform its institutions to enable the formulation and implementation of economic reforms. There is no point in announcing big reforms if the people do not trust the government and will not support the reforms.

I am an optimist because from the loud noise of India's democracy as it prepares for a momentous election in a few weeks, I hear some clear signals. The people are demanding institutions that are responsive to their needs. They are demanding governments that can deliver results. They want political parties that are in touch with people and are internally democratic too. The Congress, the BJP and the new Aam Admi Party are all trying to respond, in different ways, to the people's demand for reform of institutions.

We need a vision of our future to guide us.

The poet Iqbal had described the hope that a new vision can give. I paraphrase his poetic Urdu words. He said, 'A vision that gives hope is like the pale light on the horizon that precedes the dawn. It dimly shows a path from where I stand towards the horizon I must reach. As the light strengthens just a little more, I begin to see green shoots of grass beneath the frost on the path before my feet.'

What is our vision of our future? How will we shape our institutions of democracy and institutions of business and capitalism to create a just, inclusive, sustainable and economically vibrant society? Let me offer you a vision of an inclusive, democratic and entrepreneurial India.

In this vision, democracy will become deep and will become inclusive. Democratic governments are expected to be governments of the people, for the people and by the people.

We have the largest electoral democracy in the world. We conduct elections on a scale that no other country comes close to. Our governments are elected by the people. Therefore, we have governments of the people in our states and at the national level.

People want their governments to be for the people too. Indians are protesting that their governments are not accountable to the people. They are demanding transparency. They want to know what was done with the money that was supposed to be spent to improve public services and public infrastructure. This is the core demand of the anti-corruption movements. Therefore, governance reforms to make governments accountable to citizens have become imperative.

Deep democracy is government by the people, a democracy in which citizenship is not merely the right to vote for members of assemblies, but a democracy in which citizenship is also the active management by people of their own affairs in their communities and local bodies. Not an election-time democracy, but a deliberative democracy in which citizenship is the right to understand the rules, and to shape the rules by which society governs itself.

Here, India has a long way to go. When our elected representatives say, 'You have elected us, now keep quiet and leave it to us till we come back for your votes next time', they kill the very concept of deliberative, deep democracy.

Moreover, deep democracy requires elected and accountable governments in our villages and in urban localities. We passed the seventy-third and seventy-fourth Constitutional Amendments twenty years ago. But we have not made much progress in implementing them.

India must become an inclusive economy. I humbly submit that genuine inclusion is not achieved by handouts and by redistribution. In fact, handing out and charity reinforce the idea of exclusion. Some are In and others are Out, and it is the moral responsibility of the Ins to give to those who are Out.

Those who are excluded become genuinely included only when they have equal opportunities to earn and live dignified lives, and to contribute by their efforts, too, to the creation of the wealth of the society.

Just as institutions of government must be reformed to create an inclusive democracy, institutions of business and capitalism must be reformed to create an inclusive economy. Therefore, businesses must be not only for the people. They must also be by the people, and of the people.

For inclusion, we need innovations to provide affordable and accessible goods and services, especially at the 'bottom of the economic pyramid'. This is the business opportunity for 'profit at the bottom of the pyramid' that C.K. Prahalad wrote about, and that many entrepreneurs are pursuing. By producing products and services for poorer people, they can expand their customer base. For example, the shampoo sachet enables even poor people to buy a big company's products. The people pay. The profit from the bottom of the pyramid goes to the shareholders of the capitalist enterprise.

But this does not address the root cause of poverty. People are poor, and cannot afford to pay much, because they do not have incomes. They need jobs and incomes to lift themselves out of poverty. Therefore, they must be engaged in the processes of producing goods and services for themselves and others. And, therefore, we need innovations in production models that provide more jobs, so that business is by the people too.

Employees in enterprises owned by others have incomes, but do not share in the creation of wealth, the fruits of which go entirely to the owners. For a fuller inclusion in the benefits of growth, we need more enterprises in which the producers and workers share the wealth creation too. This requires innovations in enterprise design and governance models to shape businesses of the people.

In my vision of India, an India which is a country of over a billion democrats will also be a country of hundreds of millions of entrepreneurs and capitalists.

Indeed, this was Mahatma Gandhi's vision. His charkha was a symbol. In his vision for India, all people would be producers of the goods and services that the community and the market need. They would be earners and also owners of their enterprises, even if tiny.

Finally, in my vision, India will also be what Gurudev Tagore envisioned—a country not divided into fragments by narrow domestic walls. Let us be less argumentative and more cooperative.

Let us strive together towards the heaven of freedom—a country in which every citizen has all three freedoms: political, social and economic.

Each of us has work to do to reform the institutions we are in charge of, and in which we work. Some of us must lead and reform business corporations and other capitalist institutions. Others among us must lead and reform governments and government institutions. And many others must lead and reform institutions for democratic representation—political parties, civil society organizations and labour unions.

Who will lead?

We need leaders who have the wisdom and the courage to reform the institutions they are given to lead. As Gandhi said, we do not own institutions. We are their trustees. We must build society's trust in the institutions we lead.

I conclude with my definition of a leader. Leaders come in many shapes and they have many styles. Regardless of their shape, size and style, a real leader is one who takes the first steps towards what she or he deeply cares about.

Leaders are those who take the first steps. Not those who wait for others to lead. Great leaders have many followers because the steps they take are not towards selfish goals but towards goals that others aspire to too. The heart of leadership is a deep caring for a cause. The awakening of leadership in each of us will arise when we look into ourselves and ask what we really care about deep down.

We must look inside our hearts for what we want to make our world and our country for not only our own sakes, but for our children's too. And we must stir our human aspirations to take steps now, together, to shape the future we want.

In closing, I want to thank the parents and families of these young people who are stepping out of this institution today. I also want to thank the staff and teachers of this institution who have guided these young persons. All of you have given us future leaders for our country.

You young leaders, I urge you to shut your eyes for a moment every day. Look inside your hearts and ask what is the country you want to create in your life, a good world for you and for your fellow citizens and for the next generation too. Then through the day let your thoughts and actions be directed towards this vision.

May all our prayers be with you as you step into the wider world.

R. Mukundan

Mr R. Mukundan, managing director of Tata Chemicals Limited, joined Tata Administrative Service in 1990, after completion of an MBA from the Faculty of Management Studies, Delhi University. He is an engineer from IIT Roorkee, and an alumnus of Harvard Business School.

During his twenty-five-year career with the Tata Group, he has held various responsibilities across the chemical, automotive and hospitality sectors of the Tata Group. He is also chairman of Tata Chemicals Europe Ltd, Northwich. He has been on the executive committees of various industry forums namely, ICC, ACMA, AMAI, All India Management Association, the Board of Control for Cricket in India (BCCI) and was the chairman, western region, Confederation of Indian Industry (CII), and currently president, Employers' Federation of India.

R. Mukundan

Greetings and good morning. This is indeed is a great occasion for each and every one of you assembled here and it marks the culmination of years of toil and sweat, and also the beginning of a new journey.

At the outset, let me thank Shri. Falguni Rajkumar and Dr Amitabha De for inviting me here to share my thoughts with you, and in that I seek your indulgence.

Twenty-five years ago, I was seated where you are now and looking forward to life with enthusiasm and energy and, I must add, with a bit of naivety. It happened to be a time when everything and anything was possible, and such was the innocence of the thought. Many years later, twenty-five, in fact, I still feel the same. It is tough to retain the same energy and enthusiasm, but it is that very aspect of you that is important as you move forward. It keeps you energized and focused.

You will hear many say it is a VUCA world—volatile, unpredictable, complex and ambiguous—and you will also

Convocation address delivered by Mr R. Mukundan, managing director, Tata Chemicals Ltd, at the Indian Institute of Management Shillong, on 4 April 2015. Reproduced with the permission of the author.

hear many say it is a world full of opportunities. Both are right. When did we last hear of Uber, the world's largest taxi company with no taxis; Facebook, the world's most popular media company, which creates no content; Apple, with over two hundred million smartphones and no factory; and WhatsApp, which sees three million messages a day but does not own servers?

Disruptive innovation and collaborative consumption is shifting the lines of the economy; the digital world has made usage more valuable than ownership. That's a big fundamental shift. However, that is not the only shift you will see. There will be many more in your twenty-five years and beyond. When I joined the workforce, we had telex machines, fax machines, cyclostyling of paper, pagers and so on. Today, all this is history. I call them technology dinosaurs. We will have many more on the way.

So, with all this, how does one cope? How does one find a way? This set me thinking and I am going to speak from my life experience. It is an experience of working for one enterprise—Tata. And within Tata, many companies, but still Tata. Sometimes when I tell people that this is my twenty-fifth year with Tata, young graduates like you look at me in wonderment, as if I am one of the museum pieces. But let me assure you that monogamy in a career is as good as monogamy in marital life. But you must choose your career well, choose your firm well, just like you need to choose your spouse well.

Also, I cannot forget to mention my many indulgent bosses. It is important to have supportive mentors, gurus and superiors in an organization. They have been my pillars of strength in my journey through Tata. And what a journey it has been; after that, I had immense opportunities. That's what a good organization and mentors can provide. I thank Tata once again for being that enterprise.

When I was first invited to come here, my instinct was to immediately approach Dr De on what I should say. Then, on reflection, I did not ask him.

For, if I had asked anyone else, I would have lost the spontaneity of the moment. I would have not followed my heart and experienced the uncertainty of the moment but would have just ended up following a set of rules that I may not have been used to or liked. Hence my first point: with all that you have learnt, there is no greater joy than living in the moment and experiencing it to the fullest and facing the consequences of the same and learning even more.

Hence, if I were to wish for you something, it would be many moments of spontaneity, joy and learning. But for that, you must all do something only you can do—follow your heart (even while you think with your mind). Don't lead someone else's life; lead your own.

Lead your life you must, but with no regrets. Every choice has consequences and that we must accept as reality. Hence, when I graduated from IIT Roorkee, there was a choice to make—to go to the US or stay back in India. I simply could not bring myself to leave this country. I felt somehow indebted to this country for what it had given me. I felt obligated to work here. But I was not sure. So what do you do when you are not sure? Postpone. And postpone my decision I did. And I joined an MBA course. (I don't want anyone to think that all of you are here because you are trying to procrastinate on a decision, but I certainly was.)

Two years into the course, twenty-four years ago, I was clearer that I wanted to stay back, but I was not sure of what to pursue as a career. I did not want to be a banker (I thought there was no fun in making money by taking and giving money); I did not want to do marketing (because I thought most of the companies made people buy stuff they did not need). This tells you how confused one's mind can be. Hence, I joined the Tatas; they said you don't need to specialize and you can be a generalist. That suited me perfectly. All I can tell you is that I have never regretted the decision. Every one of my last twenty-five years has been fun and different. I have grown, and every bit of what I am is because of Tata.

That brings me to the second point: it is not important to be sure of what you want as long as you are in good company—'Sat Sangat'. You will find your true calling, but in good company you will find a noble true calling. A true test of Sat Sangat is by seeing what an organization or person has done in the past. People are creatures of habit. If a person or organization has good habits then it is surely going to be a better place and a place I would call Sat Sangat. Hence, all your life, try to surround yourself with good people. There are three simple words that the Tatas have taken as their motto from Zarathustra: *humata*, *hukhta* and *hvarshta*—good thoughts, good words and good deeds. This may not matter now, but surely when you are twenty-five years down the road, good company will be all that can keep you steady and sane.

Just another anecdote: When I was thirteen years old, my dad sent me to a typing school in summer, and I had to continue to learn typing and shorthand. I used to think he was literally nuts to make me go through this. Then one summer day I gathered enough courage to ask him why I had to do this. He looked at me and said, 'Just so that in case you don't get anywhere and can't pursue what you need in studies, you will at least have a job as a typist and stenographer.' He also used to keep an old cycle at home. I used to ask him why; he would answer that if ever we don't have enough money, then this will be the cheapest and easiest transport for us. That is my third lesson: have simple needs and wants and don't complicate your life by wanting more and more.

If your needs are simple then even if you get something or lose something you are not worried. Don't compare yourself to others in terms of bigger cars or bigger or better houses. It is nice to have them, but not necessary to have them. I ask you, who adds more value—a person who earns Rs 1 crore in a bank sanctioning loans or a district collector who earns probably half of that but takes care of the day-to-day needs of a large number of people? Hence, what matters is not the size of the purse but the size of purpose.

You will all lead. You are all the leaders of today and tomorrow. You are entering a world full of opportunities as well as difficulties. You have choices to make. The world will be a better place because of the three forces of technology and innovation, attention to sustainability and tremendous growth in talent. You have great choices in your careers as entrepreneurs and as employees. I have often wondered how we make choices between good and bad in our job and what principles to apply; but before I go there, let me spend a minute on sustainability.

We all know we have one planet and for our current needs we need one and a half planets, and if we continue on our path, we will need three planets in the next twenty years, which is not possible. Hence, we must change ourselves. I have great hope for the generations coming now into the workforce—that you will do what we could not, that you will be sensitive to the environment and society. We need to focus on energy efficiency, water efficiency, waste reduction and carbon efficiency. We really cannot escape this now. The recent extreme climatic events have shown what nature can unleash if we continue to plunder Mother Earth. In whichever firm or entity you create or work for, please take this up as the number one priority.

In addition, we cannot have the kind of difference have between the haves and the have-nots. We are all privileged and we must use our privileged position to bring about change and contribute to a more equitable world. You will have bosses who will push you for more profits and market capitalization—to squeeze juice out of every stakeholder so that the share price can move up. This single-minded attention to share prices today at the cost of long-term sustainability is the cause of the deaths of many organizations. Don't fall for that trap. I have in my own way resisted this trap of being pushed for short-term results. After all, bosses are humans; they want to look good and will push you for quarterly results. Work towards building an ethical, sustainable and happy organization; you will have long-term success. In this, the only guidepost I have is to refer to the father of our nation—Mahatma Gandhi. His principles were five:

1. Ahimsa: don't harm anyone
2. Satya: follow the truth
3. Swaraj: freedom at the individual level

4. Sarvodaya: serve all
5. Antoyodaya: serve the last person in the queue

Let these be your guideposts while making decisions and in your work and life.

To recount my five points:

1. Follow your heart (even while you think with your mind). Don't lead someone else's life but lead your own.
2. It is not important to be sure of what you want as long as you are in good company—Sat Sangat.
3. Have simple needs and wants and don't complicate your life by wanting more and more.
4. What matters is not the size of the purse but the size of purpose.
5. Let Gandhi's five principles—Ahimsa, Satya, Swaraj, Antoyodaya and Sarvodaya—be your guideposts.

Lastly, I seek your indulgence. I am going to play a Vedic chant played by George Harrison (of the Beatles) and our own great maestro, Pandit Ravi Shankarji.

The Sahanavavatu mantra is one of the *shaanti* (peace) mantras, which have their origins in the *Taittiriya Upanishad.* This mantra is often used as a 'universal' prayer to send the message of peace and prosperity. The mantra may also be used to invoke God's blessings for harmony among teacher(s) and student(s).

Aum saha navavatu,
saha nau bhunaktu

Saha veeryam karvaavahai
Tejasvi naa vadhita mastu
maa vid vishaa va hai
Aum shaạntih, shaantih, shaanti.

The meaning of the Sahanavavatu mantra

Let us together (saha) be protected (navavatu) and let us together be nourished (bhunaktu) by God's blessings. Let us together join our mental forces in strength (veeryam) for the benefit of humanity (karvaavahai). Let our efforts to learn be luminous (tejasvi) and filled with joy, and endowed with the force of purpose (vadhita mastu). Let us never (maa) be poisoned (vishaa) with the seeds of hatred for anyone. Let there be peace and serenity (shaanti) in all the three universes.

Closing prayer

Sarve bhavantu sukhinah
Sarve santu niraamayah
Sarve bhadraani pashyantu
Maa kaschit dukha abhaag bhavet
Aum shaanti shaanti shaantihi.

Translation:

May all be happy;
May all be free from diseases;
May none be subjected to misery;

May all see things auspicious;
Aum peace, peace, peace.

This is my invocation for all of you in this convocation. May you all be happy and see things auspicious. Not just that, may you all spread joy and happiness to whomever you touch. For what is the purpose of this life if not to spread happiness and joy? I wish you all a great journey ahead. And as you go on this journey, remember a quote which I have held dear to my heart, one of my favourite lines from T.S. Eliot's poem 'Little Gidding':

We shall not cease from exploration
And the end of all our exploring
Will be to arrive where we started
And know the place for the first time.

Happy journey. Thank you.

Indra K. Nooyi

Indra K. Nooyi is chairman and chief executive officer of PepsiCo.

Prior to becoming CEO, Ms Nooyi served as president and chief financial officer beginning in 2001, when she was also named to PepsiCo's board of directors. In this position, she was responsible for PepsiCo's corporate functions, including finance, strategy, business process optimization, corporate platforms and innovation, procurement, investor relations and information technology. Between February 2000 and April 2001, Ms Nooyi was senior vice president, corporate strategy and development, from 1996 until 2000, and as PepsiCo's senior vice president, strategic planning from 1994 until 1996.

Before joining PepsiCo in 1994, Ms Nooyi spent four years as senior vice president of strategy and strategic marketing for Asea Brown Boveri, a Zurich-based industrial company.

Between 1986 and 1990, Ms Nooyi worked for Motorola, where she was vice president and director of corporate strategy and planning, having joined the company as the business development executive for its automotive and industrial electronic group. Prior to Motorola, she spent six years directing international corporate strategy projects at the Boston Consulting Group. Her clients ranged from textiles and consumer goods companies to retailers and specialty chemical producers. Ms Nooyi began her career in India, where she held product manager positions at Johnson & Johnson and at Mettur Beardsell Ltd, a textile firm.

In addition to being a member of the PepsiCo board of directors, Ms Nooyi serves as a member of the boards of the US–China Business Council, the US–India Business Council, the Consumer Goods Forum, Catalyst, the Lincoln Centre for the Performing Arts and Tsinghua University. She is also a member of the foundation board of the World Economic Forum, the American Academy of Arts and Sciences and was appointed to the US–India CEO Forum by the Obama administration.

She holds a BS from Madras Christian College, an MBA from the Indian Institute of Management Calcutta and a master of public and private management from Yale.

Indra K. Nooyi

Good evening, everyone. Thank you, Chairman Balakrishnan, Director Chattopadhyay and all the deans and chairpersons of academic programmes, for welcoming me. It is great to be back at IIM Calcutta.

Graduates, proud families and loved ones, thank you so much for inviting me here to speak to you today, and congratulations on this extraordinary achievement.

As I was thinking about what I would say to you as you conclude your business education, I was reminded of an old story about a fresh MBA graduate and his father who went on a camping trip together. After hiking all day, the two men arrived at their campsite, set up a tent and fell asleep.

Some hours later, the older man woke his son. 'Look up at the sky,' he said, 'and tell me what you see.'

His son replied, 'I see millions of stars.'

'What does that tell you?' his father asked.

The MBA graduate, remembering his education, pondered for a minute.

Convocation address delivered by Ms Indra K. Nooyi, chairperson and chief executive officer of PepsiCo, at the Indian Institute of Management Calcutta, on 4 April 2015. Reproduced with the permission of the author.

'Astronomically speaking, it tells me that there are millions of galaxies and potentially billions of planets. Astrologically, it tells me that Saturn is in Leo. Meteorologically, it seems we will have a beautiful day tomorrow.'

He then turned to his father. 'Dad, what does it tell you?'

The father was silent for a moment, and then said, 'I think someone stole our tent.'

I love this story for two reasons. First, it demonstrates that an MBA degree transforms the way you view the world. The degree you are receiving today illuminates new approaches to every situation. Second, as the father reminds us, you also need to see details as well as the big picture. You can't overlook what is right in front of you.

And today, right in front of me, is a truly amazing view.

Graduates, I can see the excitement on all of your faces. I can practically hear your hearts beating with anticipation. You are about to take the next big step in your lives. Most of you are headed for your first real, well-paying jobs and, for the first time in your lives, you are not going to be dependent on anyone. It's an exciting moment, and I realize at this point I am just about all that's standing in your way!

Behind you, I can see your family and loved ones. They are glowing with pride today. They are sitting there thinking, 'It was all worth it.'

Well, let me tell you, every night they spent worrying about you, and every penny they saved for your education *was* worth it. You have exceeded their every expectation. Take it from a mother of two—there is no better feeling than the one you get watching someone you love realize their dreams.

Of course, they are hoping you will still make time for them in your busy schedules, that you will care for them in their old age, that you will use your newfound economic freedom wisely—to help them pay off debts, or hospital bills, or maybe even put some money away for your sister's wedding.

Seated around you, I see your professors and the wonderful staff of IIM Calcutta. They do this every year, but for them, it never gets old. They have invested so much in each of you. They are hoping you will go out and use your education to make a difference in society. They are counting on you to bring honour to this institution, and to make our country and our world a better place.

From where I stand, I can feel it all—the excitement, the anticipation, the pride, the hope.

There are few constants in our world; this is one of them. This is what every convocation speaker sees. And I'm sure it's what the speaker at my IIM Calcutta convocation in 1976 saw, too.

It's hard to believe that you are the fiftieth batch to graduate from IIM Calcutta. I was in the eleventh. And thinking back to my own graduation from IIM Calcutta, I can say with confidence that life here has undoubtedly changed for the better.

We didn't have the auditorium back then—our convocation was outdoors in a tiny tent on the lawn. It was not nearly as festive or as well-attended as today's ceremony.

In fact, in every way, your time here at IIM Calcutta and the world you are about to enter into is more advanced, more diverse and more global than mine was in 1976.

My batch was the first to graduate from the Joka campus. I spent my first year at the old BT Road campus, which was just an old building in the middle of Naxalite territory—not the safest area.

And when we moved to Joka, the land from here to Diamond Harbour was all empty farmlands. TKPK was actually the last town.

My batch was around a hundred students, and I was one of only five women in my class and just twelve in the whole school. They couldn't take more because there were only so many dorm rooms built for women. We talk about glass ceilings today, but back then, women were still limited by the number of *walls*.

And when it comes to resources, there is no comparison. If we got our hands on a two-year-old *Harvard Business Review*, we thought we had died and gone to heaven.

The most advanced technology available was a four-function calculator and the IBM 360 computer, which, if you've ever seen a picture, is just a giant hunk of a machine.

Needless to say, it was a different time. And India was a different place, too. When I graduated from business school, India was a great country; but back then, it was lagging behind, closed off from the rest of the world economically and socially. The only recruiting on campus was for jobs in India, and most of it was for the manufacturing sector.

For me, the dots were hard to connect, to get from that point when I graduated to where I am today. They were few and far between, and I feel blessed by the path they ultimately illuminated. For you, the dots are so numerous they form a constellation—a constellation of opportunity.

In the last forty years, the landscape has changed entirely. There are more than one hundred women graduating today, and the number of women executives on the Fortune 500 list is growing every year. India is the world's fastest-growing free-market economy and a hub of technological innovation. IIM Calcutta graduates are some of the business world's most highly sought-after recruits.

In fact, every one of you has received a placement—in record time, I'm told!—and it's safe to say you are all headed for wildly successful careers. So I'm not here to tell you how to have a successful career; I'm here to tell you that a successful career is not enough.

With the many blessings you have received, with the world-class education you have just completed, with all the incredible resources available to you right here in India, you must make something more. You must make a lasting impact.

You can change the way the world looks at business and the way business looks at the world.

You can turn the inconceivable into the inevitable.

You can leave the world a brighter, better place.

I say this, not just because it is a convocation speech and my job is to inspire you with grand pronouncements about your potential, but because as much progress as India and the world have made over the last four decades, we still have a long way to go.

We still face complex challenges like inequality, climate change and resource scarcity that demand solutions and leadership.

Making these challenges even more complex is the fact that they are all interconnected. You cannot dive into one issue without touching another.

At the same time, no issue can be contained within a particular country. Most issues you will deal with are global. You will have to learn how to take off your blinders, think expansively and realize that you are part of a global ecosystem.

It is critical that you take this responsibility seriously, because *you* are the problem-solvers and leaders we need to overcome our world's most serious challenges.

On the other hand, a number of us here today are entering the sunset of our careers. We are counting on you to make our golden years peaceful and worry-free. Bill Clinton put it so well: 'I have more yesterdays than tomorrows. You have got more tomorrows than yesterdays. And you better show up.'

I'm confident that you will show up. And, if you will allow me, I have a few suggestions to help you on your way.

Some of you may be familiar with the old career maxim: 'Learn, earn, return'.

It is the idea that successful people spend the first third of their lives developing the skills of their chosen trade, the second third maximizing their earning potential and the final third of their lives giving back through charity and mentorship of the next generation.

Today, that model is outdated.

To make an impact in a complex and fast-changing world, you must learn, earn and return—*simultaneously*—at every stage of your career. Allow me to elaborate.

I'll begin with learning. For most of you, today marks the end of your formal education—but it is only the beginning of your life's learning. If you thought you were done being a student, think again. You are a student for life.

While you have been taught how to balance a budget, you have yet to balance delivering short-term results with long-term performance at a company. While you have been taught how to manage operations, you have yet to manage the ambiguity of today's business world. While you have been taught how to market products to consumers, you have yet to market yourself within a global and ever-changing marketplace. You won't find these lessons in a textbook, but they are just as important as every discipline you have studied here at IIM Calcutta.

When you leave here today, your professors will be replaced by managers, but they will have just as much to teach you. You will be in charge of your own learning and it is a responsibility you must not take lightly.

This is my first and perhaps most important piece of advice. You know a great deal, but there is far more you do not know. So stay humble. Be curious. Read voraciously. Volunteer for hard assignments and be ready and willing to learn as you go. The higher you ascend, the more weight your decisions carry, and the more you have to learn. I got to be a CEO and, more importantly, I have stayed a CEO because I am a lifelong student.

The truth is that we live in a world of dizzying change. The best formal education cannot provide you with a lifetime's worth of knowledge. You must continue learning as you go—and that will determine *where* you go.

There is a line by the Spanish poet Antonio Machado that says it best: 'Wanderer, there is no road, the road is made by walking.' To make a lasting impact, you must make your own road. To do that, you must never, ever stop learning.

Now the next piece is the one I imagine you are all most looking forward to—earning. You are entering a world where money looms large. With a little luck and a lot of hard work, you are going to make more than a comfortable amount of it. But you must never let your net worth define your self-worth.

If you follow money in your career, you are likely to find it. But if you follow your passion, regardless of the money, you will find something more. You will find fulfilment and inspiration that will propel you further than the promise of a big payday ever could. And you will likely find money, too.

So I urge you to first find your purpose. What do you want to create in the world that isn't already there? What product, technology or service would make life better for people, and how can you make it a reality? If you can solve a problem or improve a life, even in the smallest way, your career will be worth more than any currency. And just as important as *what* you choose to do, is *how* you choose to do it.

Businesses today are largely evaluated on their short-term performance, whether quarter to quarter or year over year. But the most successful companies are not those that shine brightly for a few quarters and then quickly burn out. The most successful companies are the ones that create value over the long term—for employees, for shareholders and for the greater community. Performing in the short term is important—you won't make it to your long-term goals if you do not deliver results day-to-day.

But a company that fails to invest in future innovations, that cuts corners on environmental sustainability or short-changes community stakeholders for the sake of a few extra stock points is not going to make it for long.

My proudest accomplishment at PepsiCo is a company-wide vision I instituted when I became CEO called 'Performance with Purpose'. Performance with Purpose is our commitment to delivering strong financial results through sustainable business practices.

We are working every day to build a more balanced portfolio, to conserve natural resources and to create diverse, inclusive workplaces, because we understand that long-term growth is contingent upon a healthy relationship between a company, its community and its consumers.

Performance with Purpose is the legacy I hope to leave behind, and I urge you to start considering yours. Few people in this world are remembered for earning lots of money. So I challenge you to think bigger.

Earn respect. Earn trust. Earn a reputation for fair and thoughtful leadership. Earn a legacy you can be proud of. Because, to quote Henry Ford, 'A business that makes nothing but money is a poor business.'

To make a lasting impact, think big and build your life around long-term values, not just short-term value.

And that leads me to the final piece, returning. Today, you have accomplished something wonderful. But it is important to remember that this is not your accomplishment alone. First, it also belongs to your parents and loved ones, who have supported you, guided you and sacrificed for you. Your presence here today is proof enough that they have done their job right. So express your gratitude to them, and do it often.

Call and visit them regularly. Don't tell them you are too busy. You are not too busy. I run a Fortune 50 company and

I still call my mother two or three times every day. So, all of you can make the time.

Your parents and loved ones are your biggest advocates and best advisors. Don't ever take them for granted.

The most important lessons don't always come from the person standing in front of you; it's the people sitting behind you. So turn around for a moment please, and let's give them a round of applause.

Second, your accomplishment also belongs to your community . . . which has grounded you in faith and helped you establish your True North.

Communities are central to who we are. They shape our outlook on life, and instil values in us that last a lifetime.

They also teach us the importance of hard work and of leading a life anchored in faith and service.

No matter what you believe in, you can honour your upbringing by giving back to the towns and regions where your journeys began.

And you don't need a hefty salary to give back.

You can be a mentor to students in your hometown, or volunteer on a local development project. There's so much you can do!

Whatever you do, make it meaningful and make a difference.

Third, this honour also belongs to this institution . . . which opened its doors to you solely on the basis of your merit.

No matter your background, you had a fair and equal shot at success because of the IIMs. Your education at IIM Calcutta has opened and will open countless doors for you; now, you must endeavour to hold them open for the next batch of students.

Finally, at this pivotal moment in the history of your country, you must give back to India.

You are graduating with the skills and insights India needs to unleash its massive economic potential. You have the knowledge and the vision to identify new and unconventional solutions to old policy problems that stifle development. You can be the force that moves India to capitalize on centuries of potential and take its rightful place as a leader among nations. To make a lasting impact, you must give as much as you have received.

Graduates, looking out at you today, I am filled with hope about the future of business and the future of our world.

You have just begun the exciting, exhilarating, and at times, exhausting journey of your lives.

But you could not be better prepared for what lies ahead. So I would like to end today by sharing my wish for you as you embark on your next step.

One thing you may not know about me is that back in my college days, I had my own rock band—the LogRhythms.

I know. Looking at me now, you would never know. Like I said, the dots don't necessarily connect.

But in honour of my rock roots, I want to leave you with the words from one of my favourite songs. Because I am of the mind that Bob Dylan always says it best:

May your hands always be busy
May your feet always be swift
May you have a strong foundation
When the winds of changes shift
May your heart always be joyful

May your song always be sung
May you stay … forever young

Class of 2015, with these words in mind, go out there and get to it! I can't *wait* to see what you do.

Thank you.

Deepak Parekh

Deepak Parekh spearheads India's premier housing finance company, HDFC Ltd, which has turned the dream of owning a home into a reality for millions across the country. Parekh's astute business acumen and far-sightedness has not only made HDFC the leader in mortgages, but has also transformed it into India's leading financial services conglomerate with a presence in banking, asset management, life insurance, general insurance, real estate venture fund and education loans.

Besides HDFC Group Companies, he is the non-executive chairman of BAE Systems India (Services) Pvt. Ltd, Glaxo Smithkline Pharmaceuticals, Siemens India. He is also on the boards of Indian Hotels, Mahindra & Mahindra, Network18

Media and Investments and international boards of DP World, UAE, Vedanta PLC and on the advisory boards of several Indian corporates and MNCs.

He is dubbed as the master trouble-shooter and the unofficial crisis consultant of the government and has been a member of various high-powered advisory committees and task forces. He is associated with international organizations like the Indo–US CEO Forum, City of London and Indo–German Chamber of Commerce.

A man with a mission, Parekh's philosophy on corporate social responsibility is simple yet profound. He believes that if a company earns, it must also return to the society.

The government and industry, impressed by Parekh's performance and sobriety, have honoured him with several awards, including the Padma Bhushan in 2006, *'Bundesverdienstkreuz'*, Germany's Cross of the Order of Merit by the Federal Republic of Germany in 2014, Knight in the Order of the Legion of Honour by the French Republic in 2010, and he was the first international recipient of the Institute of Chartered Accountants in England and Wales (ICAEW) Outstanding Achievement Award 2010.

Deepak Parekh

(Mumbai, 27 April 2012)

Director Dr R. Sesha Iyer, Deputy Director Professor Abbas Ali, professors, parents, friends and students of the class of 2012, good evening. Today belongs to the outgoing students, forgive me for using the generic term 'students', because I am struggling with the alphabet soup of abbreviations—SPJIMR's PGDM, PGPM and PGEMP. If there are any letters of the alphabet that I've missed out then please attribute it purely to a generational issue. In my day, choices were very limited. You were either a graduate or a postgraduate or an MBA or a CA, the power to exercise multiple choices is what defines this generation.

Let me not digress—today is a day of great achievement; it is a new beginning; it is a moment that no one can ever take away from you. I am delighted that you chose to celebrate this momentous day with me. You have worked very hard to see this day and here you are formally attired in this blistering heat. How better a way can you students show that you have really sweated and toiled to earn your diplomas?

Convocation address delivered by Mr Deepak Parekh, chairman, HDFC Ltd, at the S.P. Jain Institute of Management and Research (SPJIMR), Mumbai, on 27 April 2012. Reproduced with the permission of the author.

I share your excitement today. Regrettably, as a student, I never got the opportunity to wear a flappy black robe, throw my tasselled square cap up in the air and scream, 'I did it!' Instead, I worked as an article clerk in the UK for an absolutely measly stipend, sat for my exams and then anxiously waited for the mail to arrive. The only indication of whether one had passed or failed was the weight of the brown envelope—a heavy one meant you passed. Despite being full of self-doubt in those days, I was fortunate to have received the heavy envelope. I can honestly say that I was never the 'bright spark'—quite the opposite, actually; I always struggled with marks. There is no chance I could ever make it as a student at an institute like yours, not with the rigorous admission procedures that you have. But this is all I want to say about myself. Today is about you and your future.

Most of the days in our lives are rather forgettable, mundane or routine, but not today. I asked myself what I could see in you students, who are by far smarter, more driven and more sophisticated than my generation ever was. Clearly, the advice I can offer you on the journey called 'life' is very little.

You already know this, but let me repeat it and say that the education that you have received from this esteemed institution gives you a head start over others. For the postgraduate diploma in management (PGDM) students, you are the much-needed new blood that will flow into the workplace. India needs your fresh ideas, new approaches and boundless energy. Armed with your education, you start out among the most fortunate. You can see how privileged you are when you recognize that a majority of your contemporaries—girls and boys in your age group in this country—have long since dropped off the education ladder.

The PGPM students are what can be termed as the 'ripe' workforce. You will now re-enter the workforce with the right blend of past work experience and a refreshed academic perspective. This combination is your new strength and employers are willing to pay a premium to recruit such people. The period of your education is akin to refuelling or recharging yourself. You now have the fire in your belly to take on new, greater challenges in your job.

And finally, the post graduate executive management programme (PGEMP) students can look forward to enhanced opportunities within their organizations. You are fortunate to work in companies that recognize the need to constantly enhance and upgrade the skills of their employees. Being a student and working simultaneously is by no means an easy task, but this juggling that you have been doing will equip you with the skills to multitask. Good leaders have to do several things at the same time, they need to know how to balance and prioritize work, and this course has put you through the drill. Your growth curve has sharpened and this in turn will ensure better productivity within your organization.

Whichever course you are graduating from today, your education from SPJIMR will always be your indelible stamp—this is the stamp of differentiation which you will carry all your life. But don't let yourself get too carried away either. Being among the best and brightest in college is no guarantee of success or failure in life. You also must remember that for most people, success takes a lot of time and patience.

I often meet various groups of students from Ivy League universities who visit India and I am shocked to note that many of these students' minds are actually being moulded into believing that if by the age of forty they are not a CEO, they are a failure. Such warped thinking is psychologically damaging and I cannot understand why certain reputed business schools are propagating such ideas. I understand that, fortunately, your institution ingrains core values as part of its curriculum and makes efforts to sensitize students to the have-nots of the world.

No doubt, the world today is a harsher place than it was ever before. The wave of economic gloom across the globe has been overpowering. A staggering number of people today are out of jobs or settling for low-paying jobs just to make ends meet. It is quite easy to get disillusioned in such circumstances. For a long time after the global financial crisis broke out, we kept saying that the Indian economy was doing fine and we would not be affected by the collapsing Western world.

In the recent period, however, India unfortunately has brought upon itself several self-induced traumas—ranging from large-scale corruption and scandals to lack of political will to push economic reforms, the inability to get our act together on policy implementation and shaking investor confidence. The problems confronting India today are critical, but I do not want to dwell too much on this since we are all aware of these issues. We can drown ourselves with negativity and doom or we can look at the bright spots, and believe me, there are many in India.

Whenever I talk to young people, I always tell them how lucky they are to be in India at this point in time. You belong to the world's largest democracy. Half of your country's 1.2 billion people are under the age of twenty-five, implying a huge and promising workforce. India will move from being the ninth-largest economy to become the fifth-largest economy by 2020. Just look at the leap that is happening in India. It took sixty years after independence to become a $1 trillion economy in 2007. India is now set to become a $2 trillion economy by 2014 and a $4 trillion economy before 2020. I believe the next decade will be a period of both great opportunity and challenge for India.

Yes, the Indian economy has slowed down, but so has the rest of the world, including all the emerging markets and the BRICS countries. India still remains the second-fastest-growing economy in the world after China. India's long-term growth story is still intact; it is just that the journey has become bumpier. India is a consumption-driven economy, the demand is domestic, and the people of this country are consuming all that is being produced and demanding more.

Look at some of the structural changes that are taking place in India that set it apart from other economies.

India accounts for 17 per cent of the world's population. Better put, one out of every six people is an Indian. So, by default, Indians are marking their footprint across the globe.

Why do you see so much consumption? The answer is India's rising middle class. Currently, India's middle class population is 250 million. This is expected to rise to 800 million by 2030.

Rapid urbanization is bringing about unprecedented changes

- 31 per cent of India' population is currently urban.
- By 2030, 40 per cent of India's population, or around 600 million people, will be living in cities and towns.

- Of course, this also means that India will need to create new cities to be able to accommodate this influx.

Affordability is driving change

- This has been seen in the Nano car, and in the tariffs on cellphones, among the lowest in the world.
- See the growth that is happening in retail and consumer loans; mortgages have grown from 1.5 per cent of banks' advances to 10 per cent of advances over the last ten years.

You may rightly ask whether I am giving you a rose-tinted vision, but the point I wish to emphasize is the future potential of India. Let me give you some numbers that speak for themselves. I like to call these numbers 'India's Big Picture'.

To see the scale of change, one has to look at a few key parameters and see the change in the years 2000 and 2010, and the projections for 2020.

- In 2000, savings as percentage of GDP were 24 per cent; in 2010, they were 34 per cent; and in 2020, they are expected to grow to 40 per cent.
- What does this mean? Higher savings translate into higher investments for the economy.
- India's literacy rate was 65 per cent in 2000, it is now 69 per cent and will reach 80 per cent by 2020.
- A more literate workforce means a more productive and skilled workforce.

- The mortgage-to-GDP ratio was 2 per cent in 2000, 9 per cent in 2010 and will rise to 25 per cent by 2020.
- This means that more Indians will be able to own homes, and at a much younger age.

Look at telecom density. In 2000, telecom density was 0.4 per cent; a decade later it rose to 68 per cent and by 2020, it will rise to 135 per cent.

- Today, mobile phones have not just changed the way we communicate, but are changing the way financial transactions are being done.
- For years, banks struggled to reach out to the remote villages, not being able to set up branches. Mobile banking will fast replace the traditional brick-and-mortar bank.
- Mobile banking may well be the best tool India has for financial inclusion.

The bottom line is that India and China are far too large for the world to ignore. Together, India and China account for 37 per cent of the world's population. A business consultancy firm estimates that consumer markets in India and China will triple over the current decade and amount to $10 trillion annually by 2020. With such staggering amounts, can any global company afford not to have a piece of the Indian pie? Yes, many investors today have India on their watch list. They say that India remains a priority for them, but they will not make fresh investments until India manages to get its house in order. Seriously, there is not very much left to mess up any more and we have no option but to start the clean-up process. My plea to you students is to remain optimistic; things will turn around, and do believe that India's best is still to come.

Before I conclude, I have a few pointers that you might like to keep as Post-its on your screens as you navigate life hereafter. It is a recipe of experience, wisdom, lessons learnt and lessons imparted. You have got to find what you love. Your work is going to fill a large part of your life and the only way to be truly satisfied is to do what you believe is great work. And the only way to do great work, imbued with as much passion and perfection you can muster, is to love what you do. If you have not found it, keep looking. Do not settle for the next best. As with all matters of the heart, you will know when you find it in the trajectory of this search; you will have to trust in something—your instinct, your destiny, life, karma, promise, whatever. This approach has never let me down; it has been the single-lane bridge from mediocrity to excellence.

Your ethical and moral fortitude will be tested, and it is very easy to get carried away. It is up to you to stay alert and not get sucked into disreputable conduct or business practices or anything else which has even the slightest whiff of impropriety. It is true that your education from this institute will definitely give you the upper hand at the beginning. But in the long run, it is your reputation that will determine how much success you ultimately achieve. The more successful you get, the higher the chances of being pulled into unethical and immoral business practices. And the most common excuse for such unethical behaviour is 'everyone is doing it'.

Always bear in mind that your reputation, once lost, is almost impossible to earn back. Please believe me when I tell you that you can have a successful business without ever greasing palms or paying a single rupee as a bribe. It requires effort, patience, tenacity and immense willpower, but it is doable. Shun shortcuts; in the long run, doing things the right way always pays.

Be a good team player. It isn't always possible to run the whole mile alone. Remember that being able to get along and work with other people is a great asset in the real world. People are important and nothing can happen without them. Stay humble, but know and believe in yourself. Humility is essential for self-preservation—it helps you to remain approachable.

People say that success has a thousand fathers, but failure is an orphan. Some failures in life are inevitable—it is impossible to live without failing at something, unless you live so cautiously that you might as well not have lived at all! Always remember, the risk of making mistakes is respected, so long as you own up to them and learn from them.

Today our lives revolve around, 'I'—the iPhone, iPad, iPod and whatever the next thing about to be invented is. We have become hyper-connected people, drowning in an information overload. Do remember once in a while to unplug yourself in order to recharge mentally. Look at real faces and expressions, talk to people face-to-face rather than texting or emailing a person who is within arm's reach. Surround yourself with people who stimulate you, who are like-minded and who make you happy. Do not get too carried away with the virtual world when the real world is at your feet.

India needs you now more than ever before—your bold ideas, your energy and passion. It needs doers, dreamers and optimists. It needs people who believe that things can get better and people who are willing to work to make them better.

It has truly been a privilege for me to share in a small part this momentous occasion in your life. I wish you all nothing but the best. Congratulations once again to the class of 2012.

Deepak Parekh

(Lucknow, 15 March 2014)

Good evening, ladies and gentlemen. It is indeed an honour for me to be here today as the chief guest for the annual convocation, 2014. I love the feeling of convocations, more so because as a student I never got a chance to be a part of this exciting ceremony. The chief guest of my 'convocation' was a postman in England, who brought with him a sealed brown envelope. A heavier envelope indicated that one had passed; a lighter envelope meant you needed to do the exams again. That was the way the Institute of Chartered Accountants in England and Wales did things in those days.

Fortunately, the postman paid me only one visit with the heavy brown envelope. Yes, luck was in my favour.

So the brown envelope it was—that was it. There were no excited parents to celebrate with and with my stipend as an article clerk being so measly, I now understand why no girl found me date-worthy either. A couple of weeks after I passed my exams, my parents, through an aerogramme,

Convocation address delivered by Mr Deepak Parekh, chairman, HDFC Ltd, at the Indian Institute of Management Lucknow on 15 March 2014. Reproduced with the permission of the author.

discovered that their son was after all, not such a loafer. Now that I've used the word 'aerogramme', you'll figure out exactly how dated I am. As for the bright, young students, you don't need to Google 'aerogramme'. I'll tell you—it's a thin, blue, foldable, gummed piece of letter paper that is sent abroad via air. Put in a different way, it was the WhatsApp or Facebook Messenger of the past generation. The only difference is the speed—that's how the term snail mail came about. Actually, another difference is that the aerogramme didn't get a valuation of $19 billion; it just led its way to virtual extinction.

Well, here you are, class of 2014. Congratulations. Last month, I read a fabulous headline in the newspapers and the reason why it stuck in my head is that these days good news is rather hard to come by. The headline went 'IIML achieves 100 per cent placement'. Doesn't this call for resounding applause? Really well done. With this entire batch being gainfully employed, thankfully no one has to literally stay hungry and stay foolish. Since you are all employed, the other good news is that we bankers can breathe easy and don't have to worry about chasing student loan defaults.

It must be a great feeling for all of you, isn't it? I am not graduating, but I feel your excitement. What is it that makes this moment so special? In the words of Taylor Swift, I can tell you're feeling 'happy, free, confused and lonely at the same time, it's miserable and magical'. You may be wondering where I got hold of the lyrics of singer-songwriter Taylor Swift, but I must tell you, she's being quoted at many convocations these days. One can never tell from where and from whom one can derive inspiration. And for the record, I'm not outdated on the music front. I'm hooking up with

3.4* after I'm done with this convocation address. In fact, I'm geared up to walk 3.4 km to the highway and tonight I'm ready to trade corporate strategy and finance for Metallica and Pink Floyd. I hope that, as you journey through life, you always keep music alive in your heart.

There will always be two moments of your student life that you will cherish. The first is the moment you discovered you made it to IIM Lucknow, and the other is right now, as you get ready to leave this institution. Time flies, but exciting times are up ahead. From this day onwards, you may no longer be students of IIM Lucknow, but hopefully you will remain students for life. Let each day be embraced with learning, unlearning and re-learning. Let your path be an exciting road of self-discovery.

You already know that you are among the fortunate few who will always have the indelible stamp of 'IIM' on you. I am quite sure that I would never make it to IIM, not even by a long shot and not even if there were twenty-nine IIMs in all twenty-nine states. I just don't know how you crack the CAT.

At work, you will have a head start because you will always have three rightly strung alphabets on your CV—IIM. You were among the chosen few, you worked hard for it and you truly deserve it. I hope you realize how privileged you are to have received this education. Few have the opportunity of being in a pole position. I guess you already know this, so let me tell you that, like every good thing, there are side effects too.

---

*The term 3.4 evolved out of a legend, albeit true. In the initial days of this campus, students would walk the 3.4 km distance to the highway. In order to keep themselves entertained, they would sing and play the guitar. This legend was kept alive by naming the college rock band 3.4.

So what are IIM ke side effects?

I am not talking about a third sequel to *Pyar ke Side Effects* and *Shaadi ke Side Effects.* Of course, I do know there is a blockbuster in the making—south Indian IIM girl meets north Indian IIM boy, they fall in love, fight, make up and live happily ever after.

More seriously, there are side effects of the IIM tag, and this is something you must learn to take in your stride.

IIM side effect 1: You may meet a colleague, who will go—'What, you are from IIM, how can you make mistakes? How can you not know?'

Your demeanour and decorum at the workplace will be judged constantly and because you are the so-called 'star recruits', the judging may be more intense and harsher. You may be exceptionally smart, but you will make mistakes because everyone makes mistakes. Remember, saying you don't know is the first step towards learning more. Live with this mantra—you don't know very much, you will never know very much, but start each day wanting to know more.

You will no doubt be recognized for your skills, but it is the right attitude that will determine how successful you are. Treat the people you work with well, be humble and be helpful. The more you share your ideas with others, the more ideas you will get. Organizations need good team players, not individuals who work in silos. This reminds me of a wonderful quote by Mahatma Gandhi, 'I suppose leadership at one time meant muscles, but today it means getting along with people.'

IIM side effect 2: You will encounter the inquisitive neighbour or acquaintance who will say, '*Beta, tu toh IIM se hai, pagaar saath figure ka zaroor hoga.*'

It's the IIM tag at play again and the media, too, loves to exaggerate salaries for placements, simply because it is headline grabbing. Never feel pressurized by this. There will always be someone who earns more than you and there are millions who earn substantially less. No one is saying that money does not matter; of course it does. But don't let this wonderful spark and energy that you leave IIM with turn to disgruntlement because you feel you deserve more *moolah*. Nothing is ever enough if you keep chasing money.

There is, however, a tendency (particularly among the brighter sparks like you) to keep job-hopping and, more often than not, the enticement is a small hike in the salary. You don't need to be like a frisky bunny rabbit jumping at every little dangling carrot. Give yourself time, establish yourself and prove your true worth. This won't happen in a few months. Let the initial restlessness settle down.

What you define as success will keep changing throughout your life. More importantly, choose the work you want to do, be happy with the people you work with, and the rewards will follow. Your work is going to fill a large part of your life and the only way to be truly satisfied is to do what you believe is great work. And the only way to do great work, imbued with as much passion and perfection as you can muster, is to love what you do. If you have not found it, keep looking.

IIM side effect 3: 'I'm a failure if I can't sell my start-up company for a billion dollars or if I don't become a CEO in five years and head a Fortune 500 company in ten years.'

I have only one piece of advice for you—patience, patience and patience. Most successful people are plodders and most successful people have failed many times. Most billionaires are two and a half times Zuckerberg's age. Ambition and drive is good to have, but don't tip the scale towards obsession. There is no corporate ladder to success and there is no glass ceiling to shatter. These are purely imaginary and they matter only to those who have done nothing worthwhile. The only thing that matters is the benchmarks you set for yourself.

I have no doubt in my mind that all of you here today hold the basic tools of success. Yet there's no escaping the fact that life will be like a roller coaster ride—a happy, thrilling, adrenalin rush, but at times scary, dangerous and queasy. You will rise from each fall and there will be many highs and lows. Life may take unexpected twists and turns and perhaps a complete somersault, but hopefully none of you will fall off the track. You'll hang in there, defying gravity. And then boom, the roller coaster ride will be done! YOLO (you live only once), in your lingo.

From a global perspective, there is a lot of debate about whether we are winning or losing more in the world today. On one hand, people are more prosperous, richer, healthier, better educated, better connected and living longer; yet, more than half the world is potentially unstable. Food prices are rising, corruption and organized crime are increasing, more people are unemployed, debt and economic insecurity are increasing and the gap between the rich and poor is widening dangerously.

Many see the world as a fixed pie—a zero-sum game, with someone's gain becoming another's loss. Some see the world as an expanding pie, growing due to new efficiencies and innovations. A few others see the world as an exponential growth of pies as they expect a world of unlimited possibilities and synergies that will create a better world. I do hope most of you here are optimistic enough to believe in unlimited possibilities.

India needs you now more than ever before—your bold ideas, your energy and passion. It needs doers and dreamers. It needs people who believe that things can get better and people who are willing to work to make them better. The country needs you not merely when the markets are up and when money is easy, but now, in testing and challenging times. We do not need magic to change this country; we carry all the power we need inside already.

You certainly need no advice from me on how to conduct yourself. But I do want to tell you that in life, your ethical and moral fortitude will be tested, and it is very easy to get carried away. It's up to you to stay alert and not get sucked into disreputable conduct, business practices or anything else which has even the slightest whiff of impropriety. In the long run, it's your reputation which will determine how much success you ultimately achieve. The more successful you get, the higher the chances of being pulled into unethical and immoral business practices. And the most common excuse for such unethical behaviour is, 'everyone is doing it'. So every time you hear that phrase, it should raise a huge, red flag.

Always bear in mind that your reputation, once lost, is impossible to earn back. There is no such thing as a temporary breach of integrity—you cannot make amends later. So do not stay in any place where doing the right thing is not an option. Work honestly, make people trust you and let them depend on your integrity. I always tell people I work with that you should never do anything that you would be ashamed of were it to become public. There is no softer pillow to rest your head on at night than a clear conscience.

Let me conclude with three little wisdom snippets on life, which I thought would be nice to share with you this evening.

1. Once, villagers decided to pray for rain. On the day of prayer all the people gathered and only one boy came with an umbrella. That's confidence.
2. Think of the feeling of a one-year-old baby. When you throw him up in the air, he laughs because he knows you will catch him. That's trust.
3. Every night we go to bed, we have no assurance that we will wake up alive the next morning, but we still have plans for tomorrow. That's hope.

Now it's time to say goodbye to the class of 2014. Each one of you will author your own story. You are going to do extraordinary things. That's confidence, trust and hope. And when you do those extraordinary things, I'm surely going to turn around and say, 'I told you so.'

Thank you and good luck.

Aroon Purie

Aroon Purie is the founding chairman and editor-in-chief of the India Today Group, India's most respected and diversified media conglomerate. The Group has more than thirty-six magazines including editions of leading international titles. Its flagship newsweekly, *India Today* and other publications are all market leaders. It also has four leading twenty-four-hour news channels including the largest Hindi news channel, seven radio stations, a newspaper and a consumer e-com shopping portal and strong digital, mobile and social media presence. Through its multiple media brands and platforms, the India Today Group reaches more than 100 million people every month.

An alumnus of the London School of Economics and a qualified Chartered Accountant, Aroon has served on the board of many prestigious institutions in India and abroad. He was chairman of the International Federation of the Periodical Press (FIPP) from 2009 to 2011 and was the first Asian to be given this honour.

A true pioneer, Aroon has been instrumental in changing the face of journalism in India and was awarded the Padma Bhushan by the President of India in 2001.

*****

Aroon Purie

Ladies, gentlemen and students who are to graduate today, I am honoured to be invited to this convocation, although, I am not quite sure why I have been given this honour.

I never went to business school and therefore, obviously, do not have an MBA like the one you learned boys and girls are going to get. I am not even really a businessman because I've spent most of my life as a journalist. This also means that, more often than not, I am at your side of this podium listening and observing. And not public speaking. So if I don't dazzle you, you'll know why.

Also, I've hardly attended any convocation, not even my own, for the simple reason that we didn't have one. I received my degree in the mail. That was at the London School of Economics. So count yourself lucky for having such a grand function.

And if you are still wondering how I am here, it is because of the irresistible persuasive powers of your chairman, Mr R.C. Bhargava, whom I have known for many decades

---

Convocation address delivered by Mr Aroon Purie, chief executive of the India Today Group, at the Indian Institute of Management Ranchi on 11 April 2014. Reproduced with the permission of the author.

and respect for all his achievements and wisdom. Plus, in life, you must know who you can't really say no to.

I notice from your batch profile that a majority of you are graduates in engineering and technology and now that you are adding an MBA—it is a deadly combination. I am sure it will prepare you well to take on any kind of job.

I wish I was as well-qualified for doing what I ended up doing. Let me tell you a little about my life. Maybe you'll find something useful in it, or I may be a very bad example for you. And that's one more reason I shouldn't be here lecturing you.

I must confess, I was one of those kids who didn't know what to do with their lives. Not like one of those precocious types, much to their parents delight, who come out of the mother's womb saying 'I want to be a doctor or an engineer'. I hope all you graduates-to-be came out saying you wanted to get an MBA more than anything else. And here you are with your dream coming true.

I did my degree in economics and then went on to become a chartered accountant. After finishing my chartered accountancy in the UK, I started working at an accounting firm there. I hated it.

To cut a long story short, frustrated by chartered accountancy, I returned to India and ended up running a commercial printing plant that my father had started by chance. It was not our family business. He had no clue about printing, and neither did I. With some common sense and some learning about business from accountancy training, I soon realized that for the printing company to make money, it must have its own dedicated work. Job printing meant there would be peaks and troughs according to the market and your pricing. The idle time was killing the profitability of the company.

That's how I got into publishing and the media to feed the press with our own work. I tried many things like publishing children's books, and even wrote some myself. In fact, our first publication was a medical journal. Then came *India Today* magazine in the mid-1970s, which you might have heard of.

Very often you don't know where success will come from. *India Today* magazine was, in fact, born out of a failure. It was first conceived as a magazine for Indians living abroad. It was not distributed in India. The overseas marketing of it was too difficult and expensive as Indians were too widely dispersed and too difficult to target. Remember, it was before the Internet, or even satellite TV. It was a failure.

After three months, we stopped sending it overseas; but before shutting it down completely, we put it in the Indian market as an experiment. The rest is history.

Now, thirty-nine years later, the India Today Group has thirty-seven magazines, four news channels, seven radio stations, more than a dozen websites and growing, a classical Indian music label, a daily newspaper and an e-commerce site. We as a group engage with close to a hundred million people in India.

I must tell you one principle I've always followed in my business—produce a great editorial product and the rest of the equation will balance. Money will follow once you have the audience. I today define the media business not as content creation but audience engagement.

Our major source of revenue is advertising, and in my career of four decades, I've never sold an ad. I've just concentrated on editorial, which I regard as the core of my business. So, at the age of thirty, I had found my calling. I loved what I was doing, even though I was trained and educated to do something else, and was not too bad at doing it.

That's the point—be excited and passionate about what you are. Not only will you be happy, but you will be successful.

I came to define happiness as doing a job you would do even if you were not paid for it. And you don't know what life is going to serve up to you, and where and when you'll find your calling. But keep looking till you do. The other lesson here is that we learn more from our failures than our successes. Also, success does not always come in One Big Thing which is going to change the world. It often comes in small instalments and then gains momentum of its own. I am often asked whether I had a grand vision of whatever little I've been able to achieve. But as you can see, there was no such thing.

Facebook, which today is valued at $145 billion, started as an effort by college boys like you to connect with their friends, and Apple with a bunch of young men in a garage who wanted computers to reach the common man.

Here in India too, young men and women like you are beginning to spot opportunities and turning them into big businesses.

The founders of Micromax were sharp enough to know that amid the towering presence of the Apples, the Samsungs, the Nokias and the Blackberrys, there was a section of the Indian mobile phone consumers that was not getting served. They grabbed the opportunity and are now ahead of everybody except Samsung in the Indian market. Their turnover has grown 500 times in five years to Rs 7500 crore. What a feat!

The promoters of redBus saw an opportunity in the chaos of bus reservation systems—and created a huge business out of it.

Chandra Shekhar Ghosh saw fortune at the bottom of the pyramid and created Bandhan, now India's largest microfinance company and soon to be a bank too. He is doing well by doing good.

None of these entrepreneurs knew they were going to change the world. They were passionate about what they were doing and believed in themselves. Plus, most important of all, they were having fun. But let me tell you being successful has its own dangers too. And that is, becoming a victim of your own success. It is one of the biggest diseases that infect successful individuals, companies and, as we are seeing, even political parties.

It breeds complacency, stagnation and most often arrogance. And like many fallen politicians you start believing your own propaganda. As the founder of Intel Andy Grove said, it always pays to be paranoid in business.

I am a great believer in global trends. What happens in developed countries sooner or later happens here in some form or the other. You have to be smart enough to catch it at the right time. Would you have imagined malls, movie multiplexes, cable TV, supermarkets, toll highways and the like in this country twenty years ago?

We in India are fortunate that we can go to the future and come back. As a wise man once said about the future, 'Your task is not to foresee it, but to enable it.'

More than that, all of you are truly a very lucky generation. You are born in an age of abundance and your opportunities are only limited by your imagination. When I was in college in the mid-1960s, there were only two models of cars made in India—Ambassador and Fiat—and they had a waiting list.

A Bajaj scooter had a waiting time of seven years, and to get a landline phone you had to wait for several years. There were only 30,000 cars made in India in 1965, and today there are 3.2 million, with over 100 models.

Then there were only two IIMs and there are thirteen today. There is so much you take for granted which didn't exist back then, like the Internet, computers, mobile phones, Google, and much else. All of you are born with a smartphone or an iPad in your hand. You are now part of a $2 trillion economy, which in public–private partnership (PPP) terms ranks as the third-largest in the world.

The Indian economy in the future is going to be driven by the force of numbers. Imagine that 1.2 billion people, with an average household of 4.8 each, want a dining table and four chairs. This means that 250 million tables and a billion chairs have to be manufactured. Look at the scale of this opportunity.

But there is something more precious than all this that my generation didn't have: a different mindset.

My parents were refugees from Pakistan. This meant insecurity, which comes from losing everything in a flash. It meant a preference to preserve rather than experiment, and it also meant being extremely risk-averse. There was a tendency to save rather than spend and EMIs were non-existent.

Risk aversion is the biggest hindrance to entrepreneurship, success and prosperity—this is true for individuals, institutions and economies. No wonder the US today is the most successful country in the world, since it supports risk like no other in the world.

Your generation has the ability, mindset and financial support to take risk. You live in a country bursting with youthful energy and entrepreneurship. By 2015 India will have 300 million Internet users and it will be the second-largest in the world. You live in an interconnected world and can launch businesses that are global from day one. Your generation's dream-to-fulfilment ratio is way higher than any generation before. And this is only a function of the great opportunities.

You have role models in flesh and blood that we didn't have. For those of you who want to drive the world's biggest corporations, you have Satya Nadella, Indra Nooyi, Anshu Jain and many others. Domestically, you have Flipkart, Infosys, Micromax and hordes of others who started with nothing but a great idea.

Right now, we are at the cusp of a big change. Not only are we certain to have a new government in about a month, that the government will almost certainly be headed by a person who will be new to Delhi's old establishment and considerably younger than our past leaders.

Over the last three days, I've travelled over 1500 km in UP and seen the great energy, restlessness and yearning for the country to surge ahead.

The demand for better governance from our leaders is the order of the day. Hopefully, the new leader will have the courage and imagination to address some of the biggest structural problems that continue to restrain the economy and entrepreneurship. Uninterrupted power, motorable roads, potable water, clean sanitation, basic education and training are the prerequisites of any functioning economy. It's a shame that the world's third-largest economy still doesn't have these.

The share of manufacturing in our GDP will fall to the lowest ever level of 12.3 per cent in 2013–14. That, too, is a shame. The rural sector, which is still home to 70 per cent of Indians, now contributes only 26 per cent of the national income. So, 30 per cent of Indians are generating 74 per cent of the country's income.

This kind of distortion cannot persist. And we wonder why we are creating an unequal society. I won't list out the solutions. We all know them. We have known them for ages. We need a leader who has the conviction and courage to implement them. Given the change ahead of us, we can allow ourselves to be hopeful.

No matter what lies ahead, you are a fortunate generation, children of an unprecedented social, economic and technological revolution.

I wish you Godspeed in your journey of life. Always be curious. And always be an adventurer. And whatever you do, do it with integrity and dignity. The world is your oyster. Go and conquer it.

Thank you.

S. Ramadorai

Mr Ramadorai has been in public service since February 2011 and is currently the chairman of National Skill Development Agency (NSDA) in the rank of a cabinet minister. The NSDA is an autonomous body which coordinates and harmonizes the skill development efforts of the government and the private sector to achieve the skilling targets of the nation. He is also chairman of the National Skill Development Corporation (NSDC), a public-private partnership arm of the Government of India for creating large, for-profit vocational institutions. In February 2011, the government had appointed him as the adviser to the prime minister in the National Council on Skill Development, in the rank of a cabinet minister. This council was subsumed into the NSDA in June 2013.

He recently retired as the vice chairman of Tata Consultancy Services Ltd, a company he was associated with, for forty-two years. He took charge as CEO in 1996 when the company's revenues were at $155 million and since then led the company through some of its most exciting phases, including its going public in 2004. In October 2009, he completed his tenure as CEO, leaving a $6 billion global IT services company to his successor to lead. He was then appointed vice chairman of TCS. Today, the company's revenues stand at US $13.4 billion for the year that ended on 31 March 2014.

Mr Ramadorai is chairman of the Bombay Stock Exchange (BSE Limited) and AirAsia (India) Pvt. Ltd. He continues to be an independent director on the boards of Hindustan Unilever Limited, Asian Paints Limited and Piramal Enterprises Limited.

Given his keen passion to work for the social sector and community initiatives, he also serves as the chairman on the Council of Management at the National Institute of Advanced Studies (NIAS) and the chairman of the Governing Board at the Tata Institute of Social Sciences (TISS). He is also the president of the Society for Rehabilitation of Crippled Children (SRCC), which is building a super speciality children's hospital in Mumbai.

In recognition of Ramadorai's commitment and contributions to the IT industry, he was awarded the Padma Bhushan in January 2006. In April 2009, he was awarded the CBE (Commander of the Order of the British Empire) by Her Majesty Queen Elizabeth II for his contribution to the growth of Indo-British economic relations.

His academic credentials include a bachelor's degree in physics from Delhi University, a Bachelor of Engineering degree in electronics and telecommunications from the Indian Institute of Science, Bangalore, and a master's degree in computer science from the University of California. In 1993, Ramadorai attended the

Sloan School of Management's highly acclaimed Senior Executive Development Program.

Ramadorai is a well-recognized global leader and technocrat who has actively participated in the Indian IT journey from its inception in 1960s to a mature industry today. Ramadorai has captured this exciting journey in a wonderfully personalized book titled *'The TCS Story . . . and beyond*, which was published in 2011 and remained on top of the charts for several months.

Among his many interests, Ramadorai is also passionate about photography and Indian classical music.

S. Ramadorai

Good evening friends,

Let me be among the first to welcome you all to the first day of the rest of your life. This is an important day—a day when you shed the comfortable cloak of academic monastery and step out, armed with knowledge and insight, into the glaring heat and light of the real economy.

For the outside world, this important day will probably merit a column in the local papers tomorrow and find its way on to local TV news tonight; but other than that, it will fade away into the myriad happenings of a nation on the run and a world where tectonic shifts are taking place. But for all of you in this room, today is a crucial moment in your life and if we were to pause and reflect deeply, its significance on a larger landscape also becomes clear.

Your graduation means that the Indian economy has just has just been gifted some brilliant minds, raring to go; some fresh adrenaline has just been pumped into the growth engine. As the finest managerial talent in the country, you do

---

Convocation address delivered by Mr S. Ramadorai, vice chairman, Tata Consultancy Services, at the Indian Institute of Management, Indore, on 30 March 2009 . Reproduced with the permission of the author.

not need me to tell you what you mean to the country and its future, especially at this time when India, and indeed the world, is going through a rare transformational experience.

I mean, in the current climate, the definitions of everything are changing—an investment banker ironing five shirts on Sunday evening is the new sign of optimism; the capital of Iceland now is . . . oh, about $2.80. (All those of you who thought of Reykjavik—keep up please!) But my favourite is the one about the US banks on the Hill in front of Congress justifying their bonuses. They told the US government, 'We still demand our bonuses; only they should be even bigger!' The government official was incredulous. 'You have got to be joking!' he replied, 'you have, between you, brought the entire banking system and the real economy to its knees!' 'Perhaps,' said the bankers, 'but name another business that has just attracted £700 billion in fresh capital in tough times like these.'

Thank you, ladies and gentlemen, for inviting me to be a part of this special event. I am delighted to be visiting IIM Indore; I have known your director, Professor Ravichandran, since his IIM Ahmedabad days. I am happy to share my thoughts with all of you on a very important day, a day when over 170 of you will graduate and make the transition to the real world.

Leadership

This unprecedented crisis has brought to centre stage the whole issue of people and leadership. How well we come out of this situation depends singularly on the leadership in business and in government that will steer individual countries out of this situation. Your generation is one to have grown up in the good times—big salaries, overseas opportunities and investment bankers waiting with offers. I am delighted to hear that this year, the entire batch has been placed, though some of our contemporaries are finding the going tough. This alone demonstrates how tough things are out there. But every crisis, as we know, throws up opportunities, and I believe that this crisis can be a period of much learning for all of us.

When people talk of the recovery and India's future growth, they are placing their confidence in you. This is not merely a lofty sentiment, but based on hard facts as seen from the reality that most of the top business leaders and academicians in the country today, and high-profile Indians overseas, are from institutions such as the IITs and IIMs. The finance minister's commitment of Rs 660 crore for setting up of seven new IIMs is a step that reiterates the same sentiment. The India that we all foresee cannot be created without the world's best managers and engineers at the helm of the engine.

So, I want to say this very clearly, what you plan, think, dream of and do will be intertwined with the future of the nation at some point in time, to some extent; you have no choice, it is the price you pay for having graduated from IIM.

Impact of the economic crisis

So what are the opportunities before you? The intention of my talk today is to share with you my thoughts on where India is headed, what we need to learn from the present crisis, what opportunities this crisis presents and what all of this means to you.

The downturn has turned the business world upside down; heroes have fallen and the so called underdogs are the new heroes. Hollywood, as usual, has fast caught on to the public sentiment. So we have slumdogs as millionaires and financial institutions playing the role of villains in blockbusters.

The unglamourous is in. Public sector banks such as SBI have risen from the dust, their perception of safety coming back to favour. Indeed, the lack of coupling in some vital areas like pension and provident funds and the Indian model of a piloted course and reliance on a domestic economy actually looks more stable than many of its more export-oriented counterparts. This is even resulting in a reverse brain drain of sorts. Your own placements reflect this trend, as seen from the tilt away from investment banking to now include education, pharma and even public sector undertakings (PSUs).

Over the past few months, I have been travelling extensively across the world; it has been very useful to get a sense of what other countries are going through and how global leaders are tackling the crisis. At the World Economic Forum, for instance, the common underlying theme was that there should be a renewed focus on the real sectors of the economy and less on financial engineering. India, China and Russia, to a lesser extent, will remain the few islands of growth in the next few years—essentially, economies that have large internal markets, and which are not terribly leveraged, will continue to grow, but the prognosis for many industries in the developed world is more pain, at least in 2009.

Emergence of ethical conduct

Ethics, good governance, some form of government control and check, especially in the banking and financial sector—these are the thoughts that are being commonly reiterated. Closer to home, the Satyam debacle brought back the realization.

Luckily for India, Dalal Street may dominate Mumbai, but not the entire landmass the way Wall Street woes have captivated the US. In my own estimate, India will have GDP growth of 5–6 per cent in the coming financial year; no one can predict when the upswing will happen, it could take a year or two. So, while we need to brace ourselves for more austere measures in the immediate term, we need to keep an eye on the longer term and be ready for the upswing and the opportunities it will present.

This is exactly the stance that a company like TCS has adopted. The IT industry, like everyone else, has been affected. So for now, we are concentrating on becoming more efficient and trimming the fat that one tends to put on during periods of hectic growth—in other words, 'lean and mean' is in. This focus on what I call 'real-time management' is not unusual, it's logical. When the external environment is not in your control, then you control what you can.

I'm sure many of you perhaps want to ask of me how the Satyam matter impacts the industry and in particular TCS. First, let me say that this in no way reflects the status of the IT industry. We are more transparent and disclose much more information than many of the multinationals; we show through metrics how we run our business. We are among the fastest firms to declare audited results, like clockwork every quarter, and among the companies who provide numbers in multiple accounting formats. At TCS, the governance values have a 140-year-old pioneering legacy. Over 60 per cent of the group's assets are held through charitable trusts, and the Tata name is a unique asset that represents leadership with trust.

TCS employees, like in other Tata group companies, commit to the Tata code of conduct at the time of joining; ethical conduct is a part of our DNA and can never be compromised. The Tata model is based on the premise that 'doing well' and 'doing good' are one and the same. The economic crisis has only revealed the solidity in this kind of thinking. TCS's work in projects of national importance such as the NREGS, the NSE and NSDL are a result of this kind of thinking, and the Tata Nano is yet another example. Today, several companies that have so far focused only on exports are looking towards India's domestic market.

Emergence of good governance

Another issue that has emerged is that of governance. How does a company ensure good governance? I would like to share with you what happens at TCS.

First, our approach is that, in the long term, we are building not just a company but an institution that creates value for our customers and other stakeholders. One cornerstone of this is the Tata business excellence model, or TBEM, which is based on the Malcolm Baldrige Awards. We document all our business processes and are assessed by a team of other group executives. The model is holistic and demonstrates how our processes lead to the business results we achieve. It keeps asking us, 'What did you learn from your processes? What have you improved?'

One of the key parts of the TBEM exercise is the review of the governance in the organization. We review and improve upon the organizational accountability of management actions, fiscal accountability, transparency in operations, selection and disclosure policies for governance board members, independence in internal and external audits, and protection of stakeholders interests as appropriate. A separate corporate governance assessment is carried out by a C-level executive along with a reputed consulting firm once in two years. The board members are interviewed to understand the operations of the board. The findings are shared in a report with the company executives and a consolidated summary is shared with the leaders of the Tata group.

Customer in focus

I believe that good governance must permeate to dealings with the customer as well, and the crisis is a time to come closer to your customer. Efficiency is big on their agenda as well. TCS addresses this squarely through its assurance of 'experience certainty', which is its brand tag line. This has an interesting origin. TCS focuses greatly on quality and dashboards to monitor our service levels. We give our customers access to a set of twenty-five metrics that we call our delivery dashboard, giving them real-time insights into our work and promoting a level of transparency that they do not see anywhere else. These metrics include time and cost overruns if any, the number of defects in the code per thousand function points, the type of effort being expended and so on. And of course, through this continuous feedback loop, we are able to make constant improvements in the levels of service delivery we provide.

India advantage

This kind of confidence in service delivery stems from our forty-year experience; our history runs parallel to India's industrialization. And history has shown us that we in India are at an advantage in withstanding the challenging times, and perhaps turning an adversity into an advantage. Austerity is a part of our DNA, being a developing country. We have lived with scarcity. This has its advantages—it forces you to make do with less, it forces you to optimize your resources, it challenges you to find creative solutions and then gives you an opportunity to test these solutions in a tough environment. If you get all of this right, you even have something to export.

Not surprising, then, that it is from India that has emerged the Rs 1 lakh car—the Tata Nano, the Rs 12,000 Simputer, refrigerators built to survive voltage fluctuations and the Chandrayaan, which, at Rs 386 crore, is the cheapest moon mission of the twenty-first century. Some of you may know about EKA; with a sustained performance of 132.8 teraflops, it is Asia's fastest supercomputer, built by Tata's Computational Research Laboratories Ltd (CRL) in Pune. Each of these is unique, indigenous and innovative. The point is that our 'non-rich' status has its advantages.

The dichotomy of the two Indians can actually fuel a new dimension of technological innovation, which can be led by IT. Cutting-edge technology is coming face-to-face with the basic challenges of education, healthcare and poverty, bringing at this cusp, a unique kind of convergence leading to a unique kind of innovation capable of impacting the world. What I find exciting is the possibilities we have in India to do this.

Every Indian sector—retail, power, utilities, energy, automotives, education, etc.—is poised for transformation and offers unique opportunities for young leaders to participate in their transformation; they offer you the opportunity to put to use your management skills. These companies offer a chance to a wider base of employees to actually be involved in creating a global entity, not just for the man on top. The general trend towards a convergence of technologies and the widespread penetration of IT and globalization has resulted in a new common set of skills in demand. So, lateral movement between industries is not only possible but even desirable; gone are the days when a 'steel' guy was for life—today, technology companies such as Apple have a non-engineer at the helm, and it is not unusual to have an engineer in the retail sector.

Corporate India is becoming professional; it is also hungry to go global in industry after industry. The scale and ambition of vision are totally different. My understanding of the youth of today is that they want more from life. Opportunities exist today in this country to create your own dream job. There is a chance for entrepreneurs to actually build world-class companies and their own future. The challenge to build something from scratch, scale it up, create enduring value for yourself and others—this is luring Indians back to India and to Indian companies.

Sectoral growth

Looking beyond the current austere times, the future promises some interesting developments. Consider some facts:

India is the fifth-largest retail destination globally. While organized retail in India is only 2 per cent of the $215 billion retail industry, it is expected to grow, driven by changing lifestyles, strong income growth and favourable demographic patterns.

FDI in infrastructure investments in India is now permitted up to 100 per cent in sectors such as roads and highways, ports, electricity generation, transmission and distribution, and industrial parks, among others. The Indian power industry, for instance, is transforming from a government-controlled PSU framework to business management in a corporate framework; the sector is seeing active participation of private players—naturally, this has created a huge demand in the changed roles of technical and managerial personnel at various levels.

Increasingly, green energy is going to drive the agenda of both governments as well as businesses. As an emerging sector, it offers huge potential for technological innovations and an opportunity worth thinking about.

India's telecommunications industry is booming—the country's mobile-phone market, adding over six million new users a month, is one of the fastest-growing in the world and presents exciting opportunities. The ministry of communications and information technology's 2010 vision aims to reach 500 million mobile-phone subscriptions, coverage of 85 per cent of the country by mobile networks, a mobile penetration rate of 90 per cent, and 80 million mobile connections in rural areas. While we are all witness to the exciting developments in this sector in our cities, the rural telephony market—huge and pregnant with opportunity—is waiting to be tapped. Telecom offers the dream of connecting the two Indians we live in—it promises to bridge the digital divide. This kind of work is certainly very different from what you would do in a swanky office handling a risk management kind of portfolio; however, it has a sweet earthy smell and offers the immense satisfaction of transforming lives.

India's future lies in the development of its tier-II cities. Cities such as Indore, Nagpur, Pune and Ahmedabad will drive the pace of our growth. Take Indore for example, it is a favoured test market for industries owing to the diversity of its population; I am aware of plans for a software park, and I saw several shopping malls during my drive earlier. Tata International, India's leading leather and leather products exporter, is based at Dewas, not far from here. In fact, it would not be wrong to say that Indore is one of the fastest-developing cities. Combine this with the fact that this city has a great supply pool, being an educational hub with good schools and engineering and management institutes, it's obvious that the city has great potential.

The best way to exploit this potential is to make it attractive enough for business to invest and managers like you opt to take the lead in grabbing the opportunities here.

India's growth must be uniform; to achieve 7 per cent growth, which is the figure quoted by our finance minister, you cannot have laggards—all sectors need to grow. Agricultural transformation is imperative, and this too needs management expertise and technology expertise. The government must invest in the rural sector and innovation efforts must look to transform productivity and other challenges peculiar to this sector; should we ignore it, it will pull down the pace of growth and negate any progress.

This pace of growth is not without challenges. Because organizations and the environment in which they operate are changing much faster than they did a few decades ago, the chasm between the skills required and skills available is widening rapidly. The needs are vast. All these developments indicate the strong need for managerial leadership, especially given the fact that not only are we competing globally, we are also acquiring globally.

I hope I have given you a sense of the size of the giant transformation we are talking about; now imagine the managerial talent this calls for collectively.

Being hands-on as a life skill

As you step into your new careers, it is useful to understand that life need not start with a bang—you have to build it step by step. Life experiences at the grass roots level help to build up a huge vocabulary that you can draw upon as you grow in your career. So, companies such as Unilever and GSK will promptly dispatch the suave MBA to the remotest rural destination to see the transformation happening there and TCS would get its software engineers to write code, and companies such as SBI may actually have their trainees deliver to desks as a way to get to know people and their functions.

At TCS, we think of ourselves as a learning organization; given that technology has a short shelf life, unlearning and learning is a survival tactic. So, from the time you join as a young engineer, you train in software tools to soft skills; deployment in projects means learning on the job, and this operational experience is invaluable later—since we work in sectors as different as banking and biotechnology, domain experience in these is vital. You are periodically encouraged to pool back all that you have learnt by opting to teach young trainees. We have a system of committing a certain minimum time of the year to learning/training for every individual as part of the growth plan. So, at every level of seniority, there are opportunities for continuous education. This forms a very solid foundation for leadership roles.

Rolling up your sleeves and getting your hands dirty has its merits. It gives you the capacity to shoulder immense responsibility from a young age, to grow as a leader among your peers, to be aware of the different forces that interact in one's work sphere, to understand the community that one works in, and to bring together the whole gamut of organizational efforts needed to make things happen. When I was setting up data centres, mainframes and other machinery that would fill this room in the 1980s, but still provide less processing power than in our laptops today, many of the decisions I made in the middle of situations laid the groundwork for me to be able to evolve as a team leader and as a mentor to my colleagues.

Conclusion

I'd like to close my talk by saying that the crisis has been a wake-up call to the world and India. While making your life choices, take a sweeping look at what is happening in the country—take up the challenge to make a real difference, there are a million opportunities everywhere, put your management skills to full use.

I ask you today, will you be one of those to join the bandwagon and take up the traditional careers that IIM students do or will you be among those that will create something unique? This is something I would like you to think about.

Whatever your decision may be, I hope you build your careers with substance—have the satisfaction of having contributed to society and having given something of your expertise for social good. This is not about making a sacrifice, it is about conducting ourselves with responsibility.

If I have managed to provoke you into thinking about what is happening in the country, the extraordinary challenges this offers you and the enormous job satisfaction that can be your reward, that alone would have been worth this journey.

Thank you.

N. Ravichandran

N. Ravichandran graduated from IIT Madras in 1980. The same year, he joined IIM Ahmedabad as a faculty in the production and quantitative methods (P&QM) area. He has taught several courses in the areas of operations research, operations management and competitive strategy. He provided transformational leadership to IIM Indore in the capacity of director from November 2008 to January 2014. He is the founder president of the Case Research Society of India (CRSI) which was created to promote the case method of teaching in Indian business schools. He has also founded a not-for-profit foundation, Management Research Foundation (MRF), to improve the quality of management education in India.

N. Ravichandran

(Indore, 30 March 2009)

Distinguished chief guest, Mr Ramadorai, respected Lakshmi Nivasji, chairman of the Board of Governors, IIM Indore, honourable members of the board, IIM Indore, the IIM Indore society, faculty and staff, guests and my dear students, it is a matter of pride that I stand before you to say a few words on the most important yearly occasion of this academic institute.

At the outset, let me join the IIM Indore community in congratulating you on the successful completion of the prestigious educational programme. In this country, education is a great differentiator. Since you are endowed with a wonderful educational experience, you have a greater opportunity to contribute to the welfare of the society and community in which you choose to work.

As you are aware, IIM Indore is entering its second decade. The unique advantage of IIM Indore, like India, is its youth.

We are endowed with outstanding students, a wonderful faculty, a great infrastructure, understanding supporting staff, an enlightened Board of Governors and a benevolent

Convocation address delivered by Dr N. Ravichandran, director at the Indian Institute of Management Indore, on 30 March 2009.

government. There is no reason why we cannot transform ourselves into an institute of national repute and international standing in the years to come.

We do not only want to see ourselves as an outstanding management institution; we also want to contribute to the resolution of important social issues in India.

We are in the process of enhancing our talented faculty's strength, streamlining the academic process and adding additional and new activities to the existing set of activities. With the support of the stakeholders of IIM Indore, I am confident that we will be able to achieve our objective of becoming one of the top five management schools in the country in the next five years.

Based on my own experience, let me add a few words of caution and advice, as you are ready to begin your journey into real life. In order to make a difference, you must be able to carefully blend fairness, smartness and innovation. The outside world is not systematically organized. Therefore, you have to be extremely cautious and careful in dealing with situations that you may have to come across in your professional life. While uprightness, transparency and frankness are important virtues, the delivery of them has to be carefully calibrated to ensure the accomplishment of the purpose, in the context of real life.

While passion will provide you with the excellence that you are striving for, compassion will provide you with an opportunity to distinguish yourself in the changing world.

Whenever you are unable to resolve an issue, use the intuition, consciousness and values that you have gained in the institute—as well as your educational experience—to resolve conflicts of major interest.

Farewell! Thank you.

N. Ravichandran

(Indore, 29 March 2010)

Distinguished chief guest, Shri. Harsh Mariwala, respected Shri. Lakshmi Nivasji, chairman of the Board of Governors, IIM Indore, members of the board, IIM Indore, honourable members of the IIM Indore society, faculty members, staff of the institute, guests and my dear students, it is a matter of great pride that I stand before you to say a few words on the most important yearly occasion of our institute, and what is perhaps the most important occasion in your professional lives.

At the outset, let me join the IIM Indore community in congratulating you on the successful completion of the prestigious educational programme. Since you are endowed with an outstanding educational experience, you have a greater opportunity to contribute to the welfare of the society and community in which you choose to work.

With profound sadness, I would like to recall the most unfortunate event that occurred on our campus during this year. However, we have been able to motivate ourselves and

Convocation address delivered by Dr N. Ravichandran, director at the Indian Institute of Management Indore, on 29 March 2010.

move ahead in our aim to redesign, reposition and re-energize this institution.

In the 2009 convocation, we set ourselves the goal of being one among the top five management schools in the next five years. I am pleased to inform you that we have a strategy and an action plan in place to get there. We are in the process of implementing several infrastructural requirements to increase our class size from 240 to 450. We are in the process of re-profiling our faculty and staff. We are streamlining the systems and procedures related to admissions, the postgraduate-programme design, and delivery and placement. We are making every effort that is possible and using every opportunity that comes our way to build the brand of IIM Indore and make it a wonderful place to stay and study.

Based on my own experience, I would like to propose a framework of five points in life, which I would call the Panchasheel.

Firstly, the institute has empowered you with knowledge and skills, but you will find that in real life, the power of compassion is more useful.

Secondly, the educational process that you have gone through should have emphasized motivation, pride and accomplishment. You will realize in life that humility and internal satisfaction are the most rewarding.

Thirdly, you will realize as you progress in your life that while others will judge you for your acts and the results, the final judgement is in your consciousness.

Fourthly, you must have appreciated the concept of ownership in the institute while you underwent your education process. You will realize that practising trusteeship is far more realistic and rewarding.

Fifthly, while attachment is good, attachment with detachment is the recipe for a satisfying and fulfilling life.

These five points may appear to be remotely connected to your experience now, but I am sure as you go further in your life, you will realize the meaning and relevance of these points.

Best wishes and farewell!

Thank you.

N. Ravichandran
(Indore, 26 March 2011)

Distinguished chief guest, Shri. M.V. Subbiah, Shri. Lakshmi Nivasji, chairman of the Board of Governors, IIM Indore, members of the board, IIM Indore and honourable members of the IIM Indore society, faculty, staff, guests and my dear students, it is a matter of great pride that I stand before you to say a few words on the occasion of the twelfth annual convocation.

At the outset, let me join the IIM Indore community in congratulating you on the successful completion of the prestigious educational programme at IIM Indore.

This convocation marks an important milestone in the evolution of IIM Indore because it is the graduation ceremony of the first full-time batch of the executive postgraduate programme (EPGP).

Before I proceed further with my short speech on this occasion, I would like to recall with profound sadness that two of our students who joined us in 2009 are not with us for the graduation ceremony of their batch today.

Convocation address delivered by Dr N. Ravichandran, director at the Indian Institute of Management Indore, on 26 March 2011.

IIM Indore is steadily moving towards becoming one of the most reputed management institutes in this country. We have adequately addressed the infrastructure-related issues to meet our postgraduate programme (PGP) expansion plan.

The increase in the batch size from 240 to 450, which makes us the single largest IIM in the country, has been administratively and academically managed without any hitches. I am glad to report that both the summer placements for 450 PGP I participants and final placements for 236 PGP II participants have been smooth and effective.

Our PhD programme has thirty-five seats and is rapidly getting stabilized academically. The response to the recently launched fellow programme in the management (industry) is very encouraging.

IIM Indore's first major activity in the commercial capital of India will begin next week. We have drawn a blueprint for our significant presence in the Gulf region. In the next 100 days, we should be able to begin some of our activities in the Gulf region.

I would like to thank my colleagues who are members of the faculty, the administrative staff, the members of the board and society, the government of India, the government of Madhya Pradesh, my friends from the industry and members of the press for their cooperation and support in building our institute as a great place to live and learn in.

In the convocation address of 2009, I chose to give the graduating class some advice on how to be effective in their professional careers. In 2010, this was refined as a five-point framework (Panchasheel) to guide the graduating class in the practical world. Today, I have chosen the theme of managing oneself for this short address.

There are broadly two approaches when it comes to conducting yourself in your professional life. One is to accept the frame of reference that is already available in terms of value systems, governance, efficiency parameters, effectiveness and so on and align yourself with the existing framework.

The second option is to develop a deeper insight into your own character and personality, and evolve a vision to contribute to change in the macro environment.

This is equivalent to saying that *sukshma*, which is the micro element, has an ability to influence *stula*, which is a macro entity. While this is technically feasible, it requires a significant amount of courage, conviction, passion, hard work and a bit of luck. Needless to say, to evolve as an outstanding individual, you need to make sure that your character and conduct are impeccable and your value systems are worthwhile. While there are several volumes of literature that are published on these, adopting and practising self-management is purely a function of your mind and mindset.

For want of a better word, I would call this a *manasthithi*, or state of mind, which determines your happiness, sorrow, anger, delight, accomplishments and disappointments in your professional and personal life.

If you can, control and take charge of your *manasthithi*, then you will be able to not only cope with the *paristhithi*, or environment (consisting of family, organization and society at large), but will be able to redefine, improve and change it.

I only hope and pray that you will be able to reach such an exalted position in your professional life.

Best wishes!

N. Ravichandran

(Indore, 31 March 2012)

Distinguished chief guest, Shri. K.V. Kamath, chairman of ICICI Bank and chairman of Infosys Ltd, respected Shri. Lakshmi Nivasji, chairman of the Board of Governors, IIM Indore, members of the board, IIM Indore and honourable members of the IIM Indore society, my fellow faculty members, staff, guests, parents of the graduating class, members of the press and my dear students, it is a matter of great pride that I stand before you to say a few words on the occasion of the thirteenth annual convocation of our institute.

At the outset, let me join the IIM Indore community in congratulating you on the successful completion of the prestigious educational programme at IIM Indore.

I am truly delighted that Shri. Kamath has been generous enough to spare his valuable time and spend half a day at IIM Indore with us as the chief guest for our thirteenth annual convocation. As you are aware, he is a distinguished graduate of IIM Ahmedabad, an iconic banker and an outstanding leader. We hope that his presence on this important occasion

---

Convocation address delivered by Dr N. Ravichandran, director at the Indian Institute of Management Indore, on 31 March 2012.

inspires several of our students to shape their careers and personalities to contribute to the society.

This convocation is a unique and distinguished one due to several reasons:

Firstly, this is the first convocation of IIM Indore in which (five) PhD students (fellow programme in management) are graduating.

Secondly, this is also a convocation in which the entire, large batch of PGP students are graduating.

Thirdly, we have increased our class size from forty-five to 450 in a span of over ten years. This is a tenfold increase in ten years.

IIM Indore is moving rapidly and rigorously ahead in becoming an outstanding institute of management in the Indian context.

During the year under review, we have launched a five-year integrated programme in management (IPM), which is an innovative and bold initiative by IIM Indore. Our international expansion at Ras al-Khaimah (RAK) in the UAE is slowly and surely getting stabilized.

Our infrastructure-development activities are in full swing. We have added several buildings and a state-of-the-art sports complex with an Olympic-sized swimming pool.

Several projects are in an advanced stage of planning and will be launched in the near future. Our faculty size has doubled in the last three years and is at fifty-three in 2012. We have recruited about 300 members of staff, which is a threefold increase in three years.

We are seriously looking into how our executive education can be strengthened in terms of its content and relevance.

All these initiatives are possible only with the support of various stakeholders of our institute, namely, the government (ministry of human resource development), the members of the society, the board of governors, faculty, staff, students and their parents. I would like to gratefully acknowledge your support.

The rapid increase in the institute's activities brings brand visibility to IIM Indore. Such growth needs to be supported by ensuring quality in our activities. It also needs constant alignment of our human resources (their attitude and ability) with the broad objectives of the institute.

We are making every attempt possible to enhance the quality of our academic programme. Some concerns related to our human resources are visible. Shortly, we plan to address them adequately in the context of our institute's priorities.

Before I conclude, I would like to share with the graduating class my thoughts on management.

As you are fully aware, management includes concepts, tools and techniques. This is taught in the regular classroom. The second element of management is developing perspectives on various issues and using these perspectives to resolve complex issues in one's own personal and professional life. It is important to note the difference between perspectives and experience. When you combine experience with knowledge, over a period of time you develop perspectives.

The third (and most important) element of management is your ability to develop harmony with yourself. When you are able to harmonize your activities with your internal self, what is guaranteed is efficiency and effectiveness in your activities.

Values, goals, missions, social responsibility and governance are secondary and tertiary consequences of such a harmonization.

At an evolved level, there have to be some structural alignments in harmonizing the self and external activities (with the positive attributes) in the larger social context.

I would strongly recommend that you use self-harmonization as a benchmark and a guiding factor in resolving issues that you may have to deal with in your professional and personal life.

Before I conclude, on behalf of the IIM Indore community, I wish you all the very best in your personal and professional life.

Farewell!

Thank you.

N. Ravichandran

(Indore, 6 April 2013)

Distinguished chief guest, honourable chief justice of India (retired), Shri. Sarosh Homi Kapadia, Shri. K.V. Kamath, chairman of the board of governors, IIM Indore, members of the board and society, IIM Indore, my fellow colleagues, staff, guests, parents of the graduating class, members of the press and my dear students, it is a matter of great pride that I stand before you to say a few words on the occasion of the fourteenth annual convocation of our institute.

Before I proceed further, on behalf of both the IIM Indore community and myself, I would like to congratulate the graduating class.

The convocation is an occasion where the director of the institute reviews and reports the performance of the institute to the stakeholders at large. We have been following a tradition of highlighting major accomplishments of the institute in the convocation and using the pre-convocation function to provide a detailed report of our activities to the community.

Convocation address delivered by Dr N. Ravichandran, director at the Indian Institute of Management Indore, on 6 April 2013.

In keeping with this tradition, I would like to highlight the following major accomplishments of IIM Indore in this year:

Firstly, we are thankful to the ministry of human resource development of the government of India for persuading Shri. K.V. Kamath to accept the chairmanship at IIM Indore. Shri. K.V. Kamath is recognized for his ability to transform organizations, both in terms of scale and scope. I am sure in the years to come, the board, society and the IIM Indore community will gain vastly from his expertise, experience and leadership.

Secondly, this is the first convocation of IIM Indore where we have a (retired) chief justice of India addressing the graduating class. Justice Kapadia, in his distinguished career, has demonstrated his ability to be an agent of change in balancing the judiciary, executive and the legislative, thereby developing an innovative frame of governance in the broader social context in India.

This convocation is unique in the history of IIM Indore since, for the first time, the classes of the postgraduate programme (our flagship) from RAK, UAE, the postgraduate programme in management for working executives (PGPMX) at RAK, UAE, and PGPMX at Mumbai, are graduating as part of our ambition to be a nationally important institution with global presence.

As in the past, we will continue our efforts to streamline the quality of education at IIM Indore and also the quality of life on our campus. We have invested a substantial amount of money in our infrastructure in the last four years. We have just begun a set of new infrastructural activities. Put together, the investment is roughly five times the capital investment of the institute in 1996. As you can see, the infrastructural activities of the institute are in full swing.

In any organization, change is usually resisted. IIM Indore is not an exception. We will do everything that is possible to carry along all our community members in the transformation process of IIM Indore.

Before I conclude, I would like to share with the graduating class my own thoughts related to their conduct in professional and personal life. By any stretch of imagination, these are not words of wisdom, but are reflections of an academician.

It is recognized that all of us are captives of our own upbringing, our family environment, the opportunities that are available to us, our attitude and our orientation. Cosmetic changes in these are easy. Significant changes in these would require effort, time and willingness.

In the earlier convocations, I have composed the last few paragraphs of my address based on a theme. In this convocation, which is my fifth, I would like to focus on my own reflections based on my recent reading of the Mahabharata, the great Indian epic by Devdutt Pattanaik. The themes of this short communication are *jaya* and *vijaya*.

Even though I had the fortune of being exposed to the epics of this country in my very early days through my grandmother—along with an early-morning breakfast, which was water-soaked rice with high-quality curd and tasty pickle—my recent reading of Pattanaik's retelling of the Mahabharata led me to think more deeply about some issues that my grandmother used to summarize as short stories.

In simple terms, jaya would mean external victory and vijaya would mean internal victory—which hence has potential to create dominance over one's self.

While external victory, *jaya*, is visible and provides recognition, the internal dominance, *vijaya*, is more satisfying, fulfilling and long-lasting.

Jaya is influenced by your own ability, the intensity of competition, opportunities that are available and quality execution of business plans. *Vijaya* is influenced by your internal benchmarking, effort, moving of goal posts, maturity, calmness, quietness of mind and well-meaning ambitions related to decisions in executing a professional plan.

Vijaya is possible only when desire, greed, anger and jealousy are understood, controlled and managed. If you engage yourself in accomplishing a golden balance between *jaya* and *vijaya*, you will bring happiness to yourself, your family, your company and the society.

Focusing on *jaya* will strengthen the foundation of corporate governance and transparency in public life, and is an effective way of discharging one's own responsibilities. Focusing on *vijaya* will also provide the much-needed maturity one needs to balance the short-term and long-term performance of organizations and individual performances.

I have sketched the consequences of balancing *jaya* and *vijaya*. As you go along in your life, I hope that you will realize the importance of this and the framework it provides you with to evolve as an outstanding individual.

Given the academic training at IIM Indore and also your own pedigree, I have no doubt that you will transform the environment in which you choose to operate, and bring glory to yourself, your family and to the institute.

Farewell!

Thank you.

Janmejaya Kumar Sinha

Dr Sinha is chairman of Boston Consulting Group (BCG's) Asia Pacific Practice. He is a member of BCG's global governing executive committee.

He works extensively with clients in the US, UK, Asia, Australia and India over a range of issues encompassing large-scale organization transformation, strategy, governance, family business issues and operations turnaround. He has been a member of various committees set up by the Government of India, Reserve Bank of India (RBI), Indian Banks' Association (IBA), and chairs the Confederation of Indian Industry's (CII) committee on financial inclusion. Besides that he has been a member of the Bihar State Industrial and Investment Advisory Council.

He writes extensively in the press and is a regular speaker at the World Economic Forum, CII, IBA, FCCI, RBI and other media events. In 2010, the *Consulting* magazine named him one of the top twenty-five most influential consultants in the world.

Prior to joining the Boston Consulting Group he worked with the RBI for several years across different departments. He has also worked briefly for the World Bank.

Dr Sinha has a PhD from the Woodrow Wilson School of Public and International Affairs, Princeton University, US, a BA and an MA in economics from Clare College, Cambridge University, UK and a BA and an MA in history from St Stephen's College, Delhi University, India.

Janmejaya Kumar Sinha

Mr Ravi Kant, chairman of the board of governors, Dr Rameshan, director IIM Rohtak, distinguished faculty, ladies and gentlemen and, most of all, the graduating batch of IIM.

It is a great privilege for me to have been asked to address you today by Mr Ravi Kant, a person whom I admire greatly. But when you think about it, giving a convocation address is an onerous duty. It comes at a time when you have completed your degree and there is not much left to say. You have been taught a lot, and that, too, at an IIM. So what more is there to say? But let me still try.

I will stay away from things you know better than me and only share some of the learnings out of my life experiences. To do so, I shall try and locate my talk in the context of the world you will grow up in and why you will have the greatest opportunity possibly in the history of mankind. So what may you consider to take advantage of

---

Convocation address delivered by Dr Janmejaya Kumar Sinha, chairman, Boston Consulting Group Asia Pacific at the Indian Institute of Management Rohtak, on 21 March 2015. Reproduced with the permission of the author.

your opportunity? I am cognizant of the fact that I come between you and your celebrations, so I will restrict myself to twenty minutes.

Just fifteen years ago, in 2000, the world was a different place. If you were to look at the world order in terms of GDP, large companies, relevant consumers, overall global interest, let me be frank, India did not matter. Actually, largely, neither did Asia. But fifteen years later, the world has changed. What are the changing numbers the IMF shows?

GDP ($ trillion)	**2000**	**2015**	**2030**
US	10.3	18.3	33
Germany	1.9	3.8	7.6
France	1.4	2.3	3.8
China	1.2	10.5	50–100
India	0.47	2	10

In just fifteen years, China grew tenfold from $1.2 trillion to 10.5 trillion, India grew fivefold from $0.4 trillion to 2 trillion, the US did not even double—it went to $18.2 trillion—Germany to $3.8 trillion and France to $2.3 trillion. So, assuming the same growth going forward, by 2030 India will go on to become a $10 trillion-dollar economy and if China just grows half as fast, it will quintuple and will go on to become a $50 trillion-dollar economy.

If India speeded up to ten times, it would be the $20-trillion-dollar economy that the prime minister talked about recently! Imagine that. This has led to great riches for some, and in India itself, the number of billionaires has grown from four to ninety and the number of companies with revenues of over a billion dollars from nineteen to 190.

You are incredibly lucky to be born when you have been. You are born into an India which is ready for take-off and which, by the time you are forty, will be the third-largest economy in the world. India will need leadership and you will need to provide it.

How do you get ready? What must you do? Most of this will have been taught to you in IIM. What I want to say today is different: I just want to share a few lessons, the first and the last in the form of stories and five others that I found in my life to be important.

1. As I walked into the auditorium, I saw a picture of the gentleman who gave the convocation address to you last year—Mr Arun Maira, who in fact was my boss at BCG in 2000. The first story is, therefore, to repeat a conversation with him in 2002 that I found very enlightening. On a journey back from the Mumbai airport to our office in Free Press House, Arun asked me (then a one-year partner) how I was doing. I told him I was not doing very well; I was getting shafted by not getting the investment in the cases I was allowed to pursue, in the teams I got and in the partners willing to support me on proposals. After hearing me for some time, he said, 'I am sorry to tell you, Janme, you are not important enough for people to get up in the morning with the thought that they will fix you today. When they get up, they want to do things for themselves. If things go wrong for you, you have got to take the initiative to find the right person to talk to. Most times things will work out, sometimes you will know why they did not and at others you may even understand that

someone made a mistake. However, don't believe they are out to get you; in fact, if you talk to them, they will try and help you. But don't go about feeling like a victim. That way, nothing will improve and you will get bitter, unhappy and get caught in the victim syndrome.' Becoming a victim is really a disaster. The lesson for me was never to feel like a victim, always to take control of my own destiny.

2. We need to be secure but hungry. Insecurity does drive people, but often in bad ways. Insecurity often leads to toxic behaviour. Our need to stay commercially hungry does not have to come out of insecurity. In fact, hunger for impact and achievement is the best way to be driven. Feel the hunger to achieve. Try and do it with business partners by building a relationship with them. This is done best on the basis of providing real value to your business partner. Such a relationship creates a strong platform and drives your commercial success on the back of client satisfaction.

3. Learn to work under short-term pressure but retain a long-term perspective. Every year is important. Having an open and clear understanding of your commercial performance expectations is important for you to succeed. It helps your firm do well, and the employees and yourself too. But the short-term pressures cannot subsume the need for a longer-term perspective for each one of you individually and for your firms and their place in the market. This is not mutually contradictory but requires you to steal time from the urgent and focus it on the long term. You need to start by focusing 15 per cent of your time on thinking and doing things for the long term. The moment you do this, you create sustainable and fulfilling platforms for yourselves and set yourself well for the future.

4. We need to be humble but self-confident. Humility encourages learning; it is also a trait appreciated by most people. But humility has to be combined with self-confidence and not diffidence. Self-confidence in what you bring and the views you hold, which are well formed, based on data and experience. It must be a self-confidence that arises out of delivered performance, but is combined with a humility that recognizes that there is always room for improvement. A self-confidence that allows you to take a stand but deliver it in a manner that is humble and matter of fact, rather than pompous.

5. We have to act like doctors but need to feel like patients. When you lead you often have to think like a doctor. Do a diagnosis. Give a prescription. But doctors give prescriptions to patients. It is easy to do things to others but hard to have them done unto ourselves. It is important that we build true empathy to understand how people subjected to our diagnosis feel. We need to imagine how we would feel in their shoes. True empathy makes us appreciate better their context, and helps us understand and anticipate their reactions better. This normally does not change what we do, but sometimes does change the sequence and tone with which we do it. Such empathy makes us a lot better at communicating what we do and even helps in actually getting it done. Leaders need empathy.

6. We need to be politically astute but not political. Unfortunately, in business, naivety is not a strength! So we need to be politically astute. We need to be navigating our way in our organizations. However, just because we are politically astute, we don't need to become political. Mahatma Gandhi

was politically very astute but was not political in a personally grasping way. He was sincere and passionate and led out of his convictions. For us, this means we need to be politically astute so that we can pursue a larger purpose and not get defeated by those who prefer the status quo and sabotage attempts at betterment and change. But we need to do this consistent with our values, with tenacity and political acuity to achieve impact.

As I come to the end of my speech and before I tell you my final story, let me just say to you again, you could not be graduating at a better time. I am jealous of you. So don't spend your entire life seeking; try instead to find yourself. Allow yourself the flexibility to be hit by a thunderbolt if it happens. But otherwise commit yourself and enjoy it. Remember that the grass is not always greener on the other side. Often, it is equally brown! It gets green with nurturing and hard work.

So finally, the last story before I let you go: This one is from my high school. When I was finishing school, my rector was a priest, Father James Cox. When I had gone to say bye to him, he said, 'Janmejaya, there are two kinds of kids I have known. There are those—and they are the large majority—that when they leave St Michaels, or even more when they pass out from St Stephen's College (where you are headed), will proudly say I graduated from Michael's or Stephen's. For a few of them, very few of them, Stephen's will say equally proudly that they graduated from Stephen's. Which one of those do you want to be?' An important question, and today I ask the same to you!

To end quite simply—be worthy of yourself and have a great life. Thank you.

M.V. Subbiah

M.V. Subbiah is a third generation member of the Murugappa family. He is the former chairman of the Murugappa Group and retired in January 2004 after forty-three years of work in the family business. Today, the Murugappa Group is a Rs 24,300-crore conglomerate with its headquarters in Chennai, India.

Currently he serves as the managing trustee of its family foundation, which operates four schools, four hospitals, a polytechnic college and a research centre for bringing appropriate technologies to the villages of India.

In the late 1960s, Subbiah turned around Carborundum Universal Ltd. In the 1970s he was responsible for turning around TI Cycles. With this background the group took over an ailing 200-year-old conglomerate EID Parry (India) Ltd which also he turned around in the mid-1980s.

Subbiah is a former president of the Association of Indian Engineering Industries, a predecessor to the Confederation of Indian Industries (CII). He has been active with various other organizations in the past, including the WORTH Trust (Workshop of the Rehabilitation of the Handicapped), the Madras Crafts Foundation and the India Foundation for the Arts.

Subbiah has been a recipient of the JRD Tata Business Leadership Award in 2002 and the National HRD Award in 1988. The University of Birmingham honoured him with a Doctor of Letters in 2010. The Murugappa family is a recipient of the Distinguished Family Business Award from IMD Lausanne in 2001. The President of India conferred the Padma Bhushan to him in the year 2012.

Subbiah studied engineering at the University of Birmingham and got his diploma in industrial administration from the University of Aston, UK. He attended the program for management development (PMD) at the Harvard Business School in 1971. After his retirement he went to the Centre for Family Enterprises at Kellogg Business School for a year's sabbatical.

M.V. Subbiah

Good evening, ladies and gentlemen.

It is my privilege to start by congratulating the graduates for their commencement from one of the finest B-schools in the country. Riding high on excitement, anxiety and nostalgia, this day is definitely one of the finest days in the life of a graduate. For their parents, it is a proud day to cherish and remember. None of this would have been possible but for the dedicated team of professors and faculty ably lead by the director of IIM Indore, Professor N. Ravichandran. I thank you, sir, for giving me the opportunity to address this extraordinary bunch of individuals. I would also like to congratulate all the professors for maintaining such high academic standards year after year. I am a firm believer that it is not the brick and mortar of a campus that makes an institution, but, it is the environment that the director and faculty provide and nurture it with—it is the research and academic excellence year after year which makes the difference. It is this unique characteristic which makes IIMs the most sought out institutions across the globe.

Convocation address delivered by Mr M.V. Subbiah, executive chairman of the Murugappa Group, at the Indian Institute of Management Indore on 26 March 2010 . Reproduced with the permission of the author.

For the graduates, this day marks a leap towards a progressive and evolving twenty-first century of India—an India that, in spite of the global financial crisis, continues to grow close to 8 per cent per year in terms of GDP. The exploding entrepreneurship, growing consumption and high savings rate continue to break the shackles of our dependency on the West. While our democracy is seen as a source of stability, the improvised agricultural sector is slowly moving towards self-sufficiency. As the world watches, our private sector continues to thrive. The surge in economic and political leaders visiting India last year reinstated the important role India will play in defining the new world order and being accepted as part of the globalization process.

While we are tempted to think of a prosperous future, the seeds of greatness and failure seem to coexist. Though I am optimistic about India's future, I constantly worry about the danger to its continuing success. Political fragmentation and caste-based politics have led to 'important' being replaced by 'urgent'.

While we boast about our surplus and let food grains rot in government warehouses, millions below the poverty line continue to starve every day. The insurgency problem has further exposed the corrosive influence of apathy and denial of basic social justice in our country. Growing corruption continues to burden the poor with an implicit tax, as its acceptance as a status quo has become the way of life. Even as future leaders, when most of you look at the mean salaries as a measure of success, I for one doubt if we are building a country which all of us will be proud of. These are systematic problems, with vested interests ignoring their existence.

Such is the socioeconomic and political scenario you will walk into, where the term 'ethical business' seems to be an oxymoron. Nowadays, we hear more about unethical practices, frauds and Ponzi schemes than ever before. The Satyam scandal, the financial crisis and the 2G scam have made it seem that business is fundamentally an unethical enterprise. It reveals that there are major tensions between business and moral life—tensions that are as disturbing as they are important. Business ethics is all about finding the right balance between performance and integrity. Success in business is seen as making profits and advancing private interest and having unlimited ambition for money, position and power. Whereas the moral life, by contrast, focuses on duties to others, and places others' interest over one's own.

Many organizations have a poor environment because they concentrate on maximizing profits without thinking about the people and processes that they adopt. Sooner or later, these businesses run into problems. When the ethical environment is poor, organizational performance suffers because of poor group dynamics, suppressing openness and communication. These, of course, are hard to measure but easily felt. The easily measured drop is the one in the yield or productivity. Overall, morale gets badly affected, leaving the organization vulnerable to setbacks.

On the other hand, businesses that are ethical stand to gain a lot—a more accurate perception of the world around, a stronger business, a sustainable enterprise and, above all, peace and mental tranquillity for people working in the business.

Failure in business occurs because people are not provided with an environment to think, plan, adapt and execute effectively as a team. Evidence suggests that this kind of capability is not talent derived, but is culturally derived and can be advanced or regressed through cultural practices. This culture not only prevents unhealthy behaviour but inspires superior reasoning and performance, greater levels of innovation and better group dynamics. Ethical enterprises become preferred employers and also tend to have more committed and mutually beneficial relationships. All these are real strategic advantages to any organization.

So how can an organization become ethical and maintain it across time?

The level of ethics in the organization is determined by its culture and values—these trickle down from the top. The bottleneck of the bottle is at the top—so unless the senior management 'walks the talk', an ethical culture cannot be created. Senior managers have to build the culture on the basis of trust and effective solutions.

As you graduate and walk into one of these organizations, you will be confronted with a number of choices, challenging your ethical and moral quotient in every possible way. Let me give you some examples:

- Status quo versus change
- Control versus empowerment
- Values versus corruption
- Science versus religion
- Inclusive growth versus profit
- Greed versus welfare
- Environment versus sustainability

These are recurring choices which will not only determine the future of this country, but also your success as business leaders and entrepreneurs. As I speak, I admit that our generation has made a lot of wrong choices. We resisted change and allowed greed and corruption to erode our roots. Over 200 years of colonial rule had a lasting impact on our generation. The British believed that they could not rule in India without creating a class of people, Indian in blood and colour, but British in taste, in opinions, in morals and in intellect. It was this belief which led to the creation of various elite services such as the Indian Civil Service (ICS), followed by the Indian Administrative Service (IAS), the Indian Police Service (IPS), the Indian Audits and Accounts Service (IAAS) and other bureaucracies. As a result, Indian society degenerated not only into groups, but also into a pseudo culture and value system.

As Mahatma Gandhi, the father of our nation, warned us, 'In casting off Western tyranny, it is quite possible for such a nation to become enslaved to Western thoughts and methods. This second slavery is worse than the first.'

In spite of the warning, no political or business leader took note of it or with the seriousness that one should have taken it.

Some sixty-odd years after Independence, as we march ahead into the twenty-first century, it becomes more important for us to understand our roots, in order to avoid the dilemma while making such a choice.

The foreign invasion for years destroyed much of our documented history. Added to that, whatever was left was misinterpreted by those who governed us. For example, most of us are led to believe that Lakshmi is the goddess of wealth. Whereas, if you look back and study the roots, she is not the goddess of wealth alone, but of welfare. Welfare talks about collective growth, whereas wealth alone reflects greed and individualism.

So it is in this context that I feel blessed and honoured to have been born in the Murugappa family. Most of my knowledge acquisition came from my family and my observation of nature around. One of the first things I learned was that a tree is as healthy as its roots. It is here that I found my grandfather, though not educated in the modern sense of the term, laid the foundation of a sustainable business over a hundred years ago.

Growing up in a joint family, we were constantly reminded of three things.

- 'Let no man you transact with lose, and then you shall not either.' I understood this was from the *Arthashastra*;
- 'Knowledge and wealth, if not shared, is useless.' This is from the *Thirukkural*; and
- The principle of fairness and firmness.

So after forty-odd years in business, I retired from the family business at the age of sixty-five, following the principle given to us by our elders, which follows the four stages of human life as given in our scriptures—*brahmachari* (bachelor), *grihasta* (family), *vanaprastham* (moving away) and *sanyasam* (renunciation). These are well-thought-out stages arrived at by our ancestors.

The concept of vanaprastham is probably the most critical to business. What happens in most businesses is that a successful leader or entrepreneur gets too attached to the business and finds it difficult to let it go. In the process of making this tough choice, no appropriate successor has been trained, putting the sustainability of an organization at risk. Our scriptures teach us to live like the melon fruit which grows on the ground. When ripe, it automatically detaches itself from the stem. Fruits that grow on trees, on the other hand, drop when fully ripe or get bitten by birds, thus getting damaged. The important lesson here is to not remain self-centred, but to think of the greater cause of the organization. Plan your succession while your feet are still on the ground.

Such philosophies have been followed in our family for generations. I believe it is such a discipline and belief which has held the family in good stead, ensuring collective growth and equal opportunity for all.

With that background, the thought I would like to leave you with is, how can we overcome the social and economic disparity in our country? How can we increase shareholders' value with inclusive growth at the same time? Can we get rid of corruption and ensure high moral and ethical business practices? The answers to these lie in us being able to understand our roots, instead of blindly following the West in aping consumerism and building unnecessary aspirations. We need to get back to our roots, develop the courage to challenge the wrong, set high moral and ethical standards and lead by example for everyone to follow.

To conclude I would like to share an excerpt of Professor Pulin Garg's interpretation of Bhishma from *Shanti Parva*:

- The nature of beauty is Order
- The nature of systems is Certainty
- The nature of structure is Security

Order, Certainty and Security define the oughts of man's existence.

It is a sad day when they break down and are replaced by shoulds, for then there is chaos and oppression.

In such times, the only way to regenerate oughts is not to defy, not to deny but define—not to resist, not to desist but to persist.

Part B

G. Narayana

Shri. G. Narayana is chairman emeritus of Excel Industries Limited, chairman and director of several companies and a mentor, contributor, educator and trainer in management.

He is a mentor to several chief executives, executives, lecturers, students, corporations, management institutions, universities, colleges, schools and social, spiritual and voluntary organizations.

He has adopted a missionary life of contributing and assisting several people to experience their own inner light and potential and for peace and harmony amongst different people and groups.

He is the author of several books and articles on management, education, leadership, life and spirituality. Most of these books are published by the Ahmedabad Management Association. He has been recognized by several awards and titles.

G. Narayana

Delivering Motivational Speeches: An Operational Guide

Motivating communication touches the mind, intellect, heart and soul, and inspires people to rise in life.

It is said, 'Speech is silver.' To make it gold is in the hands of the speaker, who, with the element called motivation, can instil that drive which leaves a sense of connectivity, enthusiasm, contentment and joy in the body, mind, intellect and spirit of the listeners.

Motivation is the power, the force which can enthuse in the listener the urge to seek knowledge and wisdom not only from external sources, but from within, through one's own experiences and realizations.

Speech is not mere talk, a verbal communication, a dialogue, language or words, but it is all these working in complete concordance and coordination in order to make sense or be meaningful to the listener on a defined or specified subject or topic.

Chairman emeritus of Excel Industries. Distinguished speaker and orator at the Ahmedabad Management Association.

Hence, a motivational speech should be able to satisfy the listener's AQ (action quotient), EQ (emotional quotient), IQ (intelligence quotient) and SQ (spiritual quotient). AQ is about actions and results, EQ is about feelings and relations, IQ is about thoughts and realities and SQ is about potentials and realizations. When the AQ, EQ, IQ and SQ of the listener experience fulfilment, it means the speaker has accomplished the purpose, that is, he has successfully motivated the audience. Thereby, he himself succeeds as a motivator. His achievement is, therefore, a result of his dedication, decision, drive, determination and destination.

Dedication: the speaker is thoroughly prepared, knows the subject well, has gathered relevant and appropriate information beforehand and has sketched an outline.

Decision: the speaker knows what to present first, when to refer to statistical information, and how to be convincing and disciplined.

Drive: the speaker presents anecdotes, parables, examples or stories to draw attention, connect with the listeners and cause excitement.

Determination: the speaker shows his own confidence and hold on the subject to be impactful and effective.

Destination: the speaker accomplishes the mission and wins applause from the motivated audience.

In other words, if the motivator is himself inspiring, encouraging, focused, enthusiastic, directive, guiding, wise, experienced, communicating, empowering, accepting and strong, then the motivated listener becomes inspired, insightful, intelligent, interactive, intention-full, intensive, intimate and instinctive.

Whether addressing a huge gathering in an auditorium or just a few people in a hall or a room, the ground rules or principles for motivating them are the same.

1. Time, timing and duration of the speech: Be in time, be on time, be before time, but never be late. Be punctual, always arrive half an hour early at the venue. Be prepared in such a way that you neither exceed the time nor draw to a close too soon.
2. Opening of the speech: Greet one and all with a smile, acknowledge the vision, mission, contribution and intentions of the organizers, recognize the co-members and dignitaries on the dais, appreciate the messages delivered by the earlier speakers (if any), and begin with a prayer and a thumping opening line on the topic.
3. References and examples: While making progress, do make reference to people, places or situations which aptly fit as examples. Refer to appropriate examples from Eastern and Western scriptures, recite verses from the Bhagavad Gita, the Mahabharata, the Ramayana, the Dhammapada, the Bible, the Quran, the Japji Sahib, Zen, the Chanakya sutras, the Tao, or any such sources. These definitely add value. Moreover, this helps the listener easily connect with the speaker. On the part of the speaker, it acts as a convincing agent. It also shows his competence, confidence, clarity and conviction.
4. Panoramic view: State the statistics (but first judge their accuracy and relevance to the topic, people, situation

and place), quote, tell short stories or even crack a joke lighten the moment (if it is getting too serious). This enables the speaker to present a broader picture of the ideas, information, knowledge and wisdom, one that the listeners can clearly cognize and accept.

5. Serious point: State challenges ahead, define goals, opportunities and destiny, and discuss approaches for converting obstructions into opportunities.
6. 'Four-way reality' model: Make learners and participants grasp the core of the subject at the body, mind, intellect and spirit levels in terms of *bhakti*, *shakti*, *ukthi* and *mukti*. Touch upon management mantras such as 'Positive, active, timely and effective', 'Time, love, truth and responsibility', 'Serve and deserve', 'Pending is ending' and 'Love is accepting people as they are and supporting them to become better', and how one can move from DOG (DisOrganized Group) to GOD (Group Organization and Direction).
7. PowerPoint presentation: If you are using PPTs, use them to show something that can create interest and draw attention to the point that is being made (do not concentrate your entire speech on it).
8. Twists and turns: Let not what you say or present be predictable. Be creative and innovative in order to modify some stories to suit the present-day situations or circumstances, especially those related to competence, core competence and win-win situations.
9. Be active (by being pre-active, proactive, process-active and post-active): Keep listeners/learners alert,

> awake, aware and conscious all throughout the session, while you involve yourself actively by asking questions, doing as you say (for example, 'Clapping in a Zen-way'), reading aloud selected passages from the book or material you have referred to and so on. Be enthusiastic and let your enthusiasm spread.

In the conclusion, summarize the important points made. Communicate your message with accuracy, brevity and clarity. Declare the intention and goal. Remind the listeners of past outstanding achievements and motivate them. Uplift the spirit of the listeners by boosting their own confidence, aptitude and gusto. Thank the participants and the organizing bodies. Express your contentment and wholehearted hope for the safe and bright future of one and all.

Observe and practise what has been said above, but remember to be stable and not stumble; sensible and not senseless; insightful and not indifferent; engaged in dialogue and not in monologue; practicable and not preachy; involved in discussion and not in debate; in agreement and not in argument; heartfelt and not hurtful; and spirited and not subjugated.

THIS IS THAT

This (motivation) is that (magnificence)

Swami Nikhileswarananda

Swami Nikhileswarananda is the head of the Vadodara centre of the Ramakrishna Mission. He graduated in chemical engineering (with honours) in 1970 and postgraduated in industrial engineering in 1972. After working for a short period as a management consultant, he renounced the world and joined the Ramakrishna Order at its headquarters at Belur Math in 1976. For eleven years he edited the Gujarati monthly *Shri Ramakrishna Jyot* published from Shri Ramakrishna Ashram, Rajkot, from 1989 to 2000. Earlier he was in Ranchi, Jharkhand, from 1977 to 1986, when he guided the rural and tribal development project, 'Divyayan Krishi Vigyan Kendra'.

Before coming to Vadodara, he was the head of the Porbandar centre for eight years. He was instrumental in constructing thirty-seven school buildings and three colonies in Porbandar district as a part of earthquake rehabilitation project and in starting the Vivekananda Institute of Value Education and Culture (VIVEC).

He tours extensively both in India and abroad preaching the universal message of Vedanta in industrial houses, management institutions and educational institutions. He has visited hundreds of educational institutions for preaching the character-building message of Swami Vivekananda and has conducted training programmes on stress management, productivity through holistic management, management of the mind, total personality development, women empowerment, happiness and peace in everyday life, mind medicine and meditation, management of everyday life and so forth.

He has participated in many inter-faith conferences.

Swami Nikhileswarananda

A Historic Speech

On the morning of 11 September 1893, the Columbian Liberty Bell in the Court of Honor of the World's Columbian Exposition in the US tolled ten times to honour what were a century ago considered the world's ten great religions: Hinduism, Buddhism, Jainism, Zoroastrianism, Taoism, Confucianism, Shintoism, Judaism, Christianity and Islam. At the same time, seven miles uptown at the Memorial Art Palace, more than sixty religious leaders from around the globe processed into the Hall of Columbus to gather in a solemn assembly.

The goal of the world's Parliament of Religions was to look at unity across the many faiths. There was the hope to create not a union of religions, but a common ground for a unity that was based on peace, mutual sharing and non-violence. The desire of the delegates was to create a future where global faiths could learn from one another and find alternatives to war.

Monk, Ramakrishna Mission. At present secretary, Ramakrishna Mutt, Vadodara.

On 11 September, after the welcome was shared, the reality of that vision of global peace came from a very brief address by Swami Vivekananda. His first five words led to spontaneous applause which lasted for two minutes and he had to patiently wait for it to finish before he continued. Those five simple words were 'Sisters and brothers of America'. His vision was centuries beyond the labels and divisions that humans have adopted to foster identity and discrimination. He looked at delegations from all the different global faiths and saw only his sisters and brothers. That has always been the key to peace in local or global communities—to let go of the labels that would separate people and overlook their common humanity. He outlined a model for peace in terms of universal acceptance for all faith groups, the sharing of freedom for all faiths, and the acknowledging of different paths to that fountain of peace that we call God, Allah, Brahman, Nirvana, the Tao or Yhwh.

Vivekananda opened the door to a new way of being on 11 September 1893. He proclaimed, 'I am proud to belong to a religion which has taught the world both tolerance and universal acceptance. We believe not only in universal toleration, but we accept all religions as true. I am proud to belong to a nation which has sheltered the persecuted and the refugees of all religions and all nations of the earth. I am proud to tell you that we have gathered in our bosom the purest remnant of the Israelites, who came to southern India and took refuge with us in the very year in which their holy temple was shattered to pieces by Roman tyranny. I am proud to belong to the religion which has sheltered and is still fostering the remnant of the grand Zoroastrian nation. I will quote to you, brethren, a few lines from a hymn which

I remember to have repeated from my earliest boyhood, which is every day repeated by millions of human beings. "As the different streams having their sources in different place all mingle their water in the sea, so, O Lord, the different paths which men take through different tendencies, various though they appear, crooked or straight all lead to Thee."'

On 11 September, Vivekananda pointed the way to global peace between all people of faith. His words reveal the three basic spiritual realizations needed for peace. Peace requires letting go of past debts and grudges; peace requires seeing the goodness of others enough to grant religious freedom to all; and peace means we have looked past all the religious brand labels to grasp that eternity has no denominations.

Vivekananda was not a naive optimist. He was well aware of the destruction caused by violent religious groups throughout history. From the suffering caused by religion in human history, he dared to hope that we would consider the blessings of peace. These are his concluding words on 11 September 1893, at the World Parliament:

'The present convention, which is one of the most august assemblies ever held, is in itself a vindication, a declaration to the world of the wonderful doctrine preached in the Gita: "Whosoever comes to me, through whatsoever form, I reach him; all men are struggling through paths which in the end lead to me." Sectarianism, bigotry and its horrible descendant, fanaticism, have long possessed this beautiful earth. They have filled the earth with violence, drenched it often with human blood, destroyed civilization and sent whole nations to despair. Had it not been for these horrible demons, human society would be far more advanced than it is now. But their time is come, and I fervently hope that the bell that tolled this morning in honour of this convention may be the death-knell of all fanaticism, of all persecutions with the sword or with the pen, and of all uncharitable feelings between persons wending their way to the same goal.'

It was only a short talk, but its spirit of universality, its fundamental earnestness and broad-mindedness completely captivated the whole assembly.

The speech of Vivekananda created such a great stir that life-size pictures of him were seen posted in the streets of Chicago. The best known and most conservative of the metropolitan newspapers proclaimed him a prophet and a seer. One of the most popular newspapers—*New York Herald*—wrote, 'He is undoubtedly the greatest figure in the Parliament of Religions. After hearing him, we feel how foolish it is to send missionaries to this learned nation.' *The Critic* of New York spoke of him as 'an orator by divine rights'. Many other leading newspapers—*Boston Evening Transcript*, *Press of America*, *Interior Chicago*, *Chicago Tribune*—were eloquent about him.

This historic speech has assumed greater importance today after 123 years. This is the age of globalization; because of the development of communication technology, the world has become a global village. Globalization has come at the economic level, but where is the global peace? Global peace cannot come till we have global civilization. Samuel P. Huntington in is his book *The Clash of Civilizations and the Remaking of World Order* has pointed out that most of the wars in recent times have actually been due to a clash of civilizations.

A global civilization cannot emerge till we say goodbye to all types of fanaticism, dogmatism, sectarianism and their offshoot, terrorism. It is in this context that the historic speech delivered by Vivekananda on 11 September 1893 assumes supreme importance; his message of universal brotherhood and harmony of religions can be neglected only at the cost of great peril. We have already paid a heavy price in the past. Is it not significant that the tragic incident of destruction of the twin towers in New York took place as a result of fanaticism on 11 September 2001, exactly 108 years after Swami Vivekananda cautioned against it? Ground Zero—the site of the destruction of the twin towers—is a constant reminder of the significance of Vivekananda's historic speech.

N. Ravichandran

Crafting Inspirational Speeches

In this short note, we present the relevance of inspirational speeches in the context of organizations, communities and societies. Often, inspirational speeches are used by leaders of communities, societies and organizations to set the agenda of action. The ability to conceive, craft and deliver inspirational speeches is an important personality trait of leaders. In this note, we set the context and identify several structural constructs by which inspirational speeches are crafted.

Oral and written communication plays a vital role in the context of families, social groups, communities, organizations and societies. Often, communication is the only means to set goals and objectives, prioritize an action plan and involve stakeholders in accomplishing the stated objectives. Leaders consistently use effective communication to persuade, motivate and inspire stakeholders. Based on historical evidence, it is evident that inspiring communication has the potential to transform the lives of individuals, improve the status of communities and change the trajectory of nations.

Professor, production and quantitative methods area, Indian Institute of Management Ahmedabad.

Persuasion-based communication is often used to change or incrementally modify the position assumed by a stakeholder. The primary objective of persuasive communication is to reduce the negative perceptions about the subject matter and inject a sense of positive orientation in the thinking of individual stakeholders.

Motivation-based communication is developed within the framework of win-win situations. It usually highlights the importance of modifying or changing the stated positions of stakeholders individually or collectively. The merits of adopting a preferred action agenda is the central theme of the communication. Motivational communication is aimed at accomplishing an overall, win-win and positive outcome in the context. Communications based on an appropriate motivational pitch can bring about a rational and meaningful transformation in the attitude and performance of the individual stakeholders.

At the other extreme, inspirational communications have the potential to bring about radical changes in the context (at the level of the individual, the community and the organization). History is full of such examples and there is no need to repeat or recollect them in this short note. Needless to say, inspirational communications can provide the much-needed spark to transform and/or revolutionize a non-action-oriented group to an aspirational action-oriented team. In that sense, inspirational speeches can set and shape the transformational agenda of stakeholders and hence enable the transformation of organizations and communities.

In the main segment of this note, we infer some attributes of crafting inspirational speeches based on the empirical evidence of about two dozen convocation addresses delivered in premier management institutions in India during 2014–15.

By nature, the convocation of a graduating class is an appropriate and apt occasion to inspire young minds. The audience is a group of accomplished individuals who are waiting to begin young professional lives. The event is characterized by a ceremonial orientation. The speaker in the convocation is invariably an accomplished individual in the Indian and global context. The information, advice and insights that the speaker shares with the graduating class are not from textbooks and are predominantly based on personal experience. Therefore, the credibility, authenticity and genuineness of the contents of the address are high.

The graduating class, which is yet to begin the celebrations recognizing the fruits of their hard work, is in a state of accomplished equilibrium. They are open to advice and suggestions, and willing to consider and experiment with new guidelines before they begin their professional life. Based on these perceptions, it is evident that convocation addresses are delivered in the most optimal conditions to make a meaningful impact on a group of accomplished young individuals.

This note is not a commentary on the addresses included in the compilation. It merely uses the addresses to infer some insights related to crafting inspirational speeches. We believe such insights related to the design and delivery of inspirational speeches would enable the younger generation to appreciate the efforts involved in these speeches and use them appropriately in their professional and personal lives.

Inspirational speeches (as evidenced by the collection in this volume) are characterized in generic terms by the following attributes:

- They motivate the audience by recognizing their accomplishments and placing the event in the context of the organization, economic environment and nation.
- They clearly compare and contrast the opportunities related to wealth creation at the time the younger generation is joining the workforce with the opportunities at the time the speaker had joined the workforce.
- Addresses are based only on personal anecdotes. Accordingly, they make an impact with the audience and provide a connect. This is reinforced by the societal stature of the speaker.
- The dominating theme of the speech is optimism. The addresses succinctly capture the evolution of the opportunities of wealth creation and societal impact in the geographical context. The speeches draw the attention of the audience to the challenges at the macro and micro levels.
- The content of the speeches vary from scholarly discourses to personal advisories and storytelling, depending on the personality of the speaker.
- A detailed attempt is made to sketch the landscape of opportunities for wealth creation and social impact. However, the dominant theme is to suggest that the members of the audience explore new employment creation opportunities (entrepreneurship).

- For motivational purposes, speakers often highlight the accomplishments of the institution which is hosting the event and provide a set of deeper thoughts for contemplation, and hence enable the young minds to plan and shape the future.
- Routinely, the speeches emphasize on doing good for society, and the need and criticality of maintaining the highest standards of personal integrity.
- The speeches are sprinkled with personal anecdotes, individual experiences, observations, learning and inspiring stories to drive home a message.
- The speeches usually deal with the contemporary issues related to economic growth, wealth creation opportunities, the transformation power of IT, entrepreneurship, the growth of the consumer class, the demographic dividend, environmental concerns, social harmony, work-life balance and so on.
- Speeches are a judicious mix of appreciating accomplishments, outlining the landscape of opportunities, providing motivation to explore and take risks, reassurances based on personal anecdotes that doing good is effective in the long run, and specific advisory comments.
- The speakers' lifelong learning is the core of the address. The thrust of the address is positive motivation.

While the attributes listed above are drawn from the sample of speeches included in the volume, they can be used as a general guideline in crafting inspirational speeches.

Madhusri Shrivastava

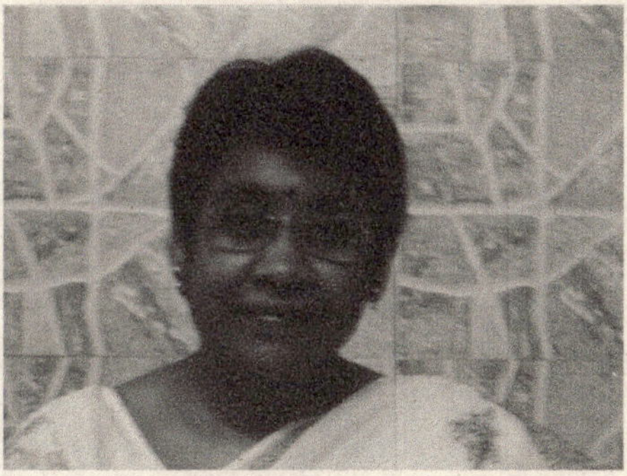

Madhusri Shrivastava is a faculty member in the area of communication at the Indian Institute of Management Indore. She has over three decades of experience in teaching business communication, mass communication, English literature and language at the postgraduate and undergraduate levels. She has a PhD in cultural studies from the department of communication and journalism, Pune University. Her areas of research interest include communication, cultural studies, literature and media studies.

She is actively involved in writing and editing books, and has written for the media as well. She conducts training sessions, workshops, faculty development programmes and executive education in effective communication and business English.

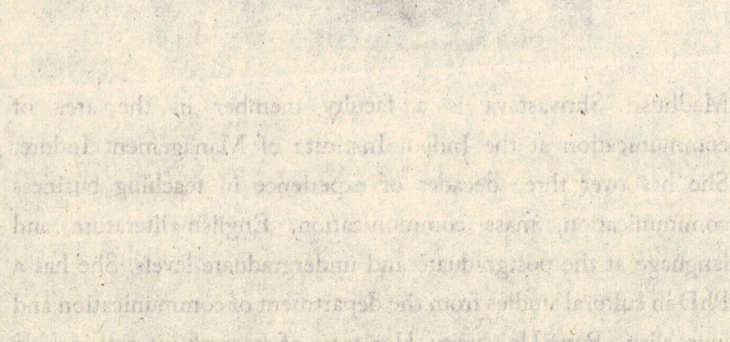

Madhusri Shrivastava

Learning from the Leaders

How do you inspire people who are cynical and resistant to change? How do you convince them to shed their inertia and embrace a world of opportunities? As a student leader you may have had your well-meaning ideas stonewalled by the very friends who chose you as their spokesperson! As a team lead, you may have tried in vain to bolster the flagging spirits of a group oblivious to its own capabilities; or else, as a young executive, you may have agonized over the best way to pitch an idea to key decision makers at your workplace. An ill-informed speaker delivering a lacklustre speech can murder the most promising plans and business deals.

Therefore, every aspiring leader must be aware of the power that can be unleashed through inspiring words. Yet, even when your efforts are well-intentioned, if you adopt the wrong approach, you could end up shooting yourself in the foot. Persuading people is both an art and a science, for it combines the sensibilities of a creative artist with the precision of a scientist. Down the centuries, words of wisdom

---

Faculty member, Indian Institute of Management Indore.

from exemplary men and women have provided the impetus for action to those poised on the cusp of transformation. From battlefields and pulpits to boardrooms and public rallies, rousing calls to action have paved the way for a brave new world.

This compilation of convocation speeches by recognized thought leaders seeks to explore the underpinnings of motivational addresses. Through an examination of speeches delivered to graduating students of premier educational institutes, it attempts to understand how leaders blend matter and manner to catalyse social change through communication. Each of the speakers is a doyen in his or her field; each has a distinctive worldview. Yet they are all united in their earnest desire to kindle a spark in young minds. As a perceptive young reader, you are sure to see a recurrent pattern in the speeches. The purpose is articulated with cogent arguments; practical advice lights up the path to realization, and the message is enlivened with hopefulness.

These remarkable similarities are not the result of a fortunate coincidence—they represent the essence of inspirational communication, and can be acquired with practice. John Collier had observed, 'Not geniuses, but average men (and women) require profound stimulation, incentive towards creative efforts and the nurture of great hopes.'* Therefore, you would do well to study how meaningful messages, communicated with conviction and confidence, can transform dreams into actuality. This book will give you a

* Cited by J. Adair 2003, in *Learning from Great Leaders: Inspiring Leadership*, Viva Books, New Delhi, p. 108.

grasp of the mainsprings of high-impact communication. The insights you gain will lay the foundation for the development of your own unique style of leadership communication.

The distillate of effective persuasion rests in ethos, pathos and logos, the cornerstones of Aristotle's exposition on the science of rhetoric. 'Ethos refers to the personality or trustworthiness of the speaker who expresses herself with integrity and reputation. Logos refers to the internal consistency of reasoning, whereas pathos is an appeal to (the audience's) emotion.'* Neither the passage of time nor shifting frames of reference have in any way detracted from these sound principles of public speaking developed by the ancient Greek masters.

To inspire is to make one act under the influence of a power greater than oneself. Unsurprisingly, at the heart of every stirring address is an overwhelming enthusiasm that inflames hearts with its irresistible force. Inspirational speeches are infused with your passionate belief in a cause, in the compelling magic of a vision. You cannot enthuse others unless you are imbued with self-belief. This belief stems from the ability to look beyond the obvious, to see in your mind's eye the shape of things to come. Your achievement lies in making the audience share dreams of a better tomorrow. The vision is thus imbibed by the audience;

---

*M. Aßländer et al. 2011. 'Pathos for Ethics, Business Excellence, Leadership and Quest for Sustainability'. *Journal of Business Ethics*, Vol. 100, No. 1, The Eben 22nd Annual Conference (April 2011), pp. 1–2. Springer. Available at: http://www.jstor.org/stable/41475823, accessed 30 March 2015 09:23 UTC.

its infinite possibilities are imagined with the concreteness of a lived reality.

How can you achieve this near miraculous feat? First and foremost, to impel people towards your preferred action, you have to establish yourself as a person worthy of the audience's time and trust. Ethos, or your believability, rests on the audience's perception of your knowledge in the chosen domain. Respect is earned when words emerge from the depth of experience and expertise. The most effective speakers prepare the ground by aligning themselves with the values that their audiences cherish. Thereafter, they introduce information relevant to the context, thus consolidating their authority as experts. Sound knowledge, personal integrity as evidenced through good moral character, and goodwill—these are the three traits that inspire confidence and induce us to repose our faith in orators even in the absence of immediate proof in their words.*

Proven success in a chosen field reinforces credibility, as does the public recognition of accomplishments. However, at the core of every successful motivational address is the ability to persuade audiences that their well-being is of paramount importance. Nothing wins over people as much as sincerity; and no argument carries as much force as that which is attuned to the needs and interests of the audience. If you wish to motivate people, you can do so only by engaging with issues that touch their lives. Effective audience analysis is thus a prerequisite to forging the all-important emotional connect.

---

* Aristotle. 350 BCE. *Rhetoric*. Translated by W. Rhys Roberts. http://classics.mit.edu/Aristotle/rhetoric.2.ii.html.

However, a mere display of knowledge cannot hold sway over hearts. To win over your audiences, clothe your message in pathos—that is, appeal to their emotions. The art of persuasion lies in deploying the right emotion to the right degree, adopting a tone that is neither offensively impersonal, nor overly sentimental. Since people respond favourably to ideas expressed with genuine warmth, your words must express positivity. Generally, we are receptive to speakers who think well of us, and are more willing to join forces with them. 'Whether they're individuals or organizations, we follow those who lead, not because we have to, but because we want to. We follow those who lead, not for them, but for ourselves.'*

Perhaps the single most important weapon in the armoury of the leader who seeks to initiate change is the art of storytelling. Stories captivate listeners and help them internalize the core message.† In her TED talk on the structure of fine presentations, Nancy Duarte posits that 'the only difference between an idea that is adopted and an idea that dies is the way it is communicated'.‡ A master storyteller wraps the message in a story that strikes a chord in the hearts of listeners, conjuring up for them a future brimming with opportunities.

---

* Simon Sinek, TED Talk. Available at: http://www.ted.com/talks/simon_sinek_how_great_leaders_inspire_action?language=en#.

† Aaker Jennifer et al. 2012. How to *Harness Stories in Business*. Stanford Graduate School of Business. https://cb.hbsp.harvard.edu/cbmp/product/M354-HCB-ENG).

‡ N. Duarte. 2012. The Secret Structure of Great Talks. TED Talks. Available at: https://vialogue.wordpress.com/2012/02/09/ted-nancy-duarte-the-secret-structure-of-great-talks/.

Yet, there is more to inspiration than merely projecting an image of happiness. Resources lie untapped within people till, with a few well-chosen words, you unlock their potential. For this to be possible you must empower them by having faith in their ability to act as carriers of your vision and affirming the importance of the task ahead. If you can make them identify with the troubles and subsequent triumphs of the hero of your story, you are well on your way to success. A word of caution here—fanciful stories may fascinate, but will not stand scrutiny unless supported by facts. Only when optimism is founded on the bedrock of pragmatism can it fuel the imagination and trigger action.

You may possess integrity and passion, but if the speech lacks logos—namely, the ballast of rational, reasonable arguments—all your emotional appeals will fail to initiate action. No matter how beneficial the message, unless the purpose is conveyed with clarity, it will leave no lasting impression. A call to action acquires relevance only when supported with illustrations; hence, good speakers make effective use of visual imagery.

Not only do they strengthen their arguments with facts and quotes, they also create word-pictures that resonate in minds long after the words themselves have faded from memory. Further, in order to achieve greater clarity, they divide messages into main points or generalizations.* In this age of reduced attention spans, it is all the more necessary

---

* W. Kelley. 1973. 'Speak the speech, I pray you'. *Improving College and University Teaching*, Vol. 21, No. 4, Academia Alive (Autumn, 1973), pp. 287–88. Taylor & Francis, Ltd. Available at: http://www.jstor.org/stable/27564593, accessed 30 March 2015 09:28 UTC.

for your speech to have a well-defined structure, wherein similar ideas are organized into groups. Meandering, long-winded talks and unplanned presentations are self-defeating. Use transitional phrases to knit sections together in a seamless flow of logic, concluding on a note of confidence and hope. The content and the context may be the blood and the bones of the message, yet it is the craft that makes the message concrete. In sum, paying scant attention to technique may prove counterproductive!

Reams have been written about the impact of non-verbal communication on audiences. Undoubtedly, your voice and appearance, your expressions and gestures contribute significantly to the way your listeners perceive you. Personal magnetism is an added advantage—it is that indefinable quality that endears you to the audience. However, you would do well to remember that some of the most inspiring speakers have not been gifted with stunning looks or even striking personalities. They are simply men and women who have wanted the best for their people, and have shown them the way to reach out for it. In the final analysis, if your words ring true, and are in tune with the aspirations of your audience, you will inspire and lead.

Part C

Debolina Dutta

Debolina Dutta has twenty-three years of work experience in HR and sales domain. She has a degree in electrical engineering from College of Engineering, Pune, a postgraduate degree in management from IIM Bangalore, and completed her FPM (Industry) programme from IIM Indore.

She is working as director-head of HR, VF Brands (I). She has over eighteen years' experience in organizational development (OD) and HR strategic initiatives in employee life cycle processes, leadership development, talent acquisition, engagement and retention and business partnership; she is also a certified practitioner of SHL (occupational personality questionnaire) assessments, Thomas PPA, PAPI psychometric solutions. She is a DDI-certified facilitator for DDI training curriculum with substantial experience in dealing with large international stakeholders in organization growth initiatives, mergers and acquisitions and multiple overseas client interfacing. OD interventions include major organization transformation initiative with human resource information systems (HRIS) implementation, project management and development of a structured talent management framework using CEB-SHL assessment solutions.

Her multiple responsibilities have included stints as business HR head for over 1000+ employees, responsible for execution of HR core processes and solutions, driving employee engagement and values through common HR themes, increase performance management effectiveness, identification of hi-pots through a calibration process, succession planning and learning investment for enhancing overall competency level of multiple business units. She has also headed the talent acquisition function at fast-moving consumer goods (FMCG) and IT majors and been responsible for campus and lateral intake, resource plans and budgeting.

Debolina contributes to academic research. Her contributions have been published by Harvard Business Publishing and Ivey Publications and other research journals.

Debolina Dutta

Reflections on Compelling Communication

For a student, the convocation ceremony is the formal culmination of a phase of life and a prelude to the changes to come. The general mood around all convocation ceremonies reflects a high level of pride among students and their families, camaraderie among students nostalgic over gruelling days of studies and fun, and a sense of excitement about the impending change this formal ceremony will bring to their lives.

The expectation, therefore, from a keynote address is a message which will build on this mood and exhort the graduating students to build on the foundations established by the school. Most keynote speakers are persons of repute who have achieved personal and professional excellence. The expectation from the institutes is that in a ten-to-fifteen minute discussion, the speaker will succinctly provide those pearls of wisdom which he or she, by dint of personal experience, deems valuable and which will guide and motivate the students in their years ahead.

Director, head of HR, VF Brands (I), Bengaluru.

Can any keynote address cover all of this, without losing the plot terribly? It truly seems a tall order. As Mr Subroto Bagchi asked '. . . do students really listen to the speech?'; to which the response was, 'they listen to be inspired and one cannot inspire enough!'

So, does inspiration happen without building a personal connect with the audience? Clearly not.

Empathy with the audience, therefore, becomes crucial for the keynote address. All memorable convocation addresses stand out since the guest speaker first demonstrates this understanding in spades. We see a similar level of empathy in opening paragraphs of Mr Ajay Banga's address to the students of IIM Ahmedabad. As an alumnus of the same institute, he understood the effort, the unflagging levels of perseverance required, the tremendous sense of competitiveness among a breed of students who epitomize excellence and, more importantly, the expectations upon graduating from such a prestigious institute that family members, faculty and the institute place on them, and that the students place on themselves. Mr Bagchi demonstrated a similar level of empathy in understanding the anxiety and emotions of the graduating class. However, this is not always established by speakers, and sometimes their speeches thereby lack the elements of connect and inspiration.

We are a country that has a rich heritage of storytelling—from our famous epics to the still relevant Panchatantra stories. What makes all of these endearing and enduring over a period of time is how they remain powerful and evergreen in firing our imagination and conveying morals without bringing in elements of sermonizing. A similar level of connect through storytelling has to be the hallmark of a powerful convocation speech, which can happen only when the speaker shares his or her learnings from anecdotes based on personal experiences. Mr Anand Mahindra demonstrated this beautifully through an anecdote exhorting students to take calculated risks. Mr Aroon Purie did the same when he advised students to pursue their passions, and said that money would follow.

Many times, unless the speaker is able to link elements of his personal experience to the address, the learnings do not emerge. It is similarly seen that personal anecdotes and instances of failure shared by eminently successful people help in reinforcing a powerful message—that it is OK to fail, but more important to learn from it, develop the courage to get up and demonstrate the resilience to try again. Sometimes, a speaker may start the discourse by stating that he or she would be sharing learnings from their experiences, but the message essentially degenerates into a distillation of all competencies of leadership, sans any personal anecdote that demonstrates how these were relevant to the speaker. These speeches clearly lack the ability to inspire, since the elements of empathy and connect are not established.

In such a context, clarity of purpose and the aim of the message has to be unambiguous. Mr Banga's message is about the discovery and awareness of the inner resilience that the school fosters, and he proposes that this resilience should give each student the confidence to face any adversity in the future. Additionally, he interweaves attributes of leadership that he would expect both in himself and the students, which will contribute to their future success. A similar level of inspiration is provided by Mr Bagchi, who reinforces the student's self-confidence in their ability to deal with change and uncertainty by citing how they have magnificently managed the same over the last few years, and exhorts them to embrace life with the same levels of courage and resilience.

Conciseness is critical to not puncture the students' enthusiasm and ensure that the key message stays with the audience long after the event is over. My personal memory of attending painfully rambling discourses has been the amusement at the sight of the fidgeting dignitaries sitting on the dais trying to hide their obvious boredom, while the audience is clearly mentally absent while being physically present. Crisp and concise messaging has been the hallmark of Dr Ravichandran's addresses, something very few speakers have been able to emulate successfully.

Modifying the message according to the audience is a principle tenet of communication, which many speakers tend to ignore. A one-size-fits-all approach, therefore, may make the audience want to head for the hills. Some speakers deliver an address which could well be presented to a forum of NGOs, an industry seminar, a body of economic policy formulators or a graduating batch of students! The effectiveness and impact of such a speech on the students is clearly as permanent as the RAM of a computer.

A critical ability of any powerful communicator is the knack of weaving humour into a speech. While one may argue that a convocation is as solemn an event in the life of the students and the institute as can be, truly memorable addresses are those where humour has carried the day, even the self-deprecating humour as indicated by Mr Purie. Similarly, whether he talked about the 'brown envelope', the 'relief to the bankers', or the 'IIM ke side effects', Mr Deepak Parekh was powerfully able to drive his message home, while engaging his audience a 100 per cent. Much like the Jataka tales, they are lessons delivered in a humorous fashion, which stay with us and remain alive in our memories.

Therefore, to deliver a truly memorable convocation speech, which inspires, motivates and remains alive and relevant, my vote is strongly in favour of including humour in the speech. Clearly, this requires an innate skill, and much like Jinnah's attempt at humour,* as recounted through the anecdote of 'Rose between two thorns', misdirected attempts at humour can go woefully awry. Barring a few, like Mr Parekh or Mr Purie, many speakers are, therefore, wary to venture down this path. Maybe the balancing act of maintaining the solemnity of the occasion and engaging an audience through humour without offending any sensibilities is what makes speakers wary of using this powerful tool.

Having attended a couple of convocations, I am unfortunately, not able to recollect what the key message by the speaker was during those important hours of my life. Reflecting on which convocation addresses have been truly memorable and inspiring (and which I had the pleasure of watching only on the Internet), the principles cited above, in my opinion, were the hallmark of all those speeches.

* *Freedom at Midnight*, Delhi, Reprint 1996, p. 100.

Sundaravalli Narayanaswami

Sundaravalli Narayanaswami has earned her PhD in industrial engineering and operations research from IIT Bombay, after a master's in computer science. Her teaching interests are in intelligent transportation systems, operations research (OR) in public systems, operations management, urban transportation, in addition to management information systems and knowledge management. Most of her research in the past and present are in transportation operations and knowledge management that involve applications of ICT and OR tools in real-life problems of large impact.

Dr Narayanaswami started her career in IT services marketing and she soon moved to a production profile in an electronics equipment manufacturing industry. Her academic career began in 1996 and she has taught at various programmes in Mumbai

University and at institutes under the UAE federal education ministry in Abu Dhabi and Dubai. She has also taught in many executive development programmes while at UAE. She publishes and reviews regularly for scholarly editorials and presents her research findings among peers, both in India and abroad. She is a life member of several professional associations and holds a fellowship from the British Computer Society. She also serves on the editorial board of the Annals of Management Science.

Dr Narayanaswami is affiliated with the public systems group of the Indian Institute of Management Ahmedabad.

Sundaravalli Narayanaswami

Inspire, Motivate and Influence: A Perspective

I got a little contemplative on who inspires and brings about a radical change in the thought process of any human being. As a woman with a classic Indian upbringing, my thoughts led me to 'mata, pita, guru'.

This is the order of importance when it comes to one human influencing another's thoughts, deeds and speech, and perhaps the journey of life. Some make a deeper impression so as to permanently change the outlook of others. As a faculty of higher education in modern times, with a plethora of opportunities and challenges in our daily lives, we often realize that we have imperceptibly influenced a few of our students' lives—imperceptibly, because we are trained not to expect rapid changes to happen, in spite of the goodwill and openness in student–faculty interactions these days.

The struggles of a faculty are mostly inward and introspective—more is not merrier any more in these changing times and various contexts; the younger generation would rather have that precise piece of processed advice that

Faculty, Indian Institute of Management Ahmedabad.

they could actually put into action rather than sieve through a flood of words and sentences. This is exactly where the crisp relevance of a convocation address lies. The second most important factor is the personality who delivers the convocation speech. We are speaking of people who have brought in some significant, unparalleled changes in their own domains of expertise and are revered as role models by large sections of society. The third is the occasion. Being a mother, I would like to relate a convocation ceremony to the moment when a baby is born. This happens only after a long gestation period (the duration of which is quite predictable) of pressures, perspiration, sleepless nights, anxieties regarding dos and don'ts, and anticipation, all of which are now over. There is also a new bundle of excitement, achievement and hope, and you have something to look forward to. And there is your society, your family and friends who cheer and welcome your promotion. At the same time, society's expectations of you change forever; they are no longer merely materialistic. Your responsibilities have grown, and you must now mature and evolve as an individual.

This compilation and dissemination of the recent convocation addresses is timely in the Indian context, in every sense. It reflects the world's hope for the Indian youth and also instils a sense of responsibility in our young population. I try to present here an overall summary of all the talks, rather than discuss individual speeches. A common message in most of them is that we must be prepared to embrace changes in the emerging world of opportunities. Young graduates are strongly encouraged to move out of their comfort zones, experiment, take risks and explore limits. They are urged to think of the growth and development of the nation, particularly rural India, but act globally with a strong consideration for ethics and integrity. The future is demanding of leaders of the world economy with Indian values and perspectives; therefore, the graduating students are urged to cater to future needs with their immense energy, enthusiasm, intuition and creativity. They need to transform organizational and individual competencies into economic progress, social welfare and sustainable growth, and bring in accountability in governance with immense urgency.

In addition to their acquired learning from the esteemed institutes, the tools that are available to our youth in such pursuits have never been more exciting. There have been unforeseen advances in technology, communication and infrastructure that allow for innovation, intuition and the stretching of horizons of creativity. The major challenge is being able to manage both successes and failures with equal grit and tenacity. Needless to say, our country has tremendous scope today for business and social growth because of our demographic diversity, democratic governance and growing supply of qualified, young citizens to cater to the global demands.

I also appreciate the fact that most of these speeches are able to connect with a diverse audience, and that their relevance is not just limited to young people who are graduating. To me, some of the speeches are very persuasive; they force everyone to introspect and look into their past and present, and they offer much-needed clarity in taking steps to achieve their future aspirations as well as personal goals.

Computer-savvy technologist that I am, I performed a small text-mining experiment on the compiled list of convocation speeches. I intended to generate a word cloud, and I present it here for the readers.

The word cloud is a semantic testimony to my descriptive reflections of the convocation speeches. However, I would also like to understand the relevance of such motivational talks as the decades flow by. I would implore to know the relevance of convocation speeches delivered during the yesteryear in the current context as much as the relevance of today's speeches in the future years. I am sure many great people are able to think beyond their times; otherwise social growth, progress and development may not have been a reality at all.

Apart from the men and women of wisdom who have been instrumental in bringing changes to the world, there is also another section of people that deserves a mention. I am speaking of those whom we meet in our daily lives who are still not known to the larger society, but make a difference in the lives of the people that they come across. In conclusion, it is my privilege to borrow words from the father of our nation—those words that precisely define inspiration: 'My life is my message.'

Bapuji has spoken these words on behalf of too many great men and women, including those many faces that the world may not ever know. It is precisely this statement that redefines the notion of inspiration.

Balaraman Rajan

Balaraman Rajan is an assistant professor at California State University (CSU) East Bay. After completing his MBA at IIT Madras he received his PhD in business administration (operations) from the Simon School of Business at the University of Rochester in 2014. He worked with a team consisting of Parkinson's disease (PD) specialists on the implementation of telemedicine to treat PD patients. The research led to his dissertation on the topic 'The Economics of Telemedicine'. He continues to work in the application of telemedicine to manage other chronic conditions like migraine and diabetes. He has an avid interest in healthcare operations and works on modelling physician time allocation and appointment scheduling systems. His work has been published in both management journals and medical journals. He has a bachelor's degree in mechanical engineering.

Besides his research, Balaraman is passionate about teaching. He has taught courses on statistics, quantitative techniques and operations management. He has been given the responsibility to steer the healthcare operations track at CSU.

He loves playing volleyball and casual hiking. He is also an occasional blogger.

Balaraman Rajan

My reflections are in two parts. The first part is as a teacher who looks for ways to engage the students and keep them focused. The second part is as a person who has just begun his academic career and looks forward to contribute something to society.

Reflections on public speaking in general

I have always wondered what makes great speakers sustain the audience interest for a long time. I think one way is by relating to them—great speakers make you feel that they are just like you, though they are not and have reached great heights. They make you feel that they had thoughts and experiences similar to yours. And that immediately brings a connection. It brings you closer to them and you start paying attention. Of course, there are other elements, like humour and intonations, but relating to the audience is one way to captivate them.

Second, there is an obvious difference between reading and listening. While you can take time to read the material

Assistant professor at California State University, East Bay.

and even have the opportunity of going back and reading it again, speeches do not have that advantage. The delivery and the receipt of the information happen simultaneously. So, the concepts, especially the heavy ones, speakers try to convey have to be put in simple sentences. Accordingly, great speakers use words that a listener will be able to retain and recall later to investigate further and absorb. The suggestions and the words of wisdom given by the speakers in this book were simple, but when you reflect on them, they tend to extend in several dimensions.

They give very simple analogies. For instance, when R. Gopalakrishnan called success a thief, it made us think. He makes us realize that in order to avoid getting 'fooled' by success, we should be able to return it and not focus on retaining it. We can extend this perspective to focus on the broader context of success. This kind of a view not only relieves the constant pressure to succeed, but also eliminates the arrogance that comes with success.

I was also able to relate to M.V. Subbiah's analogy on how we should be like the melon fruit and not be self-centred. I would like to extend this analogy to note that a teacher has to be accessible to students by staying grounded. Often, I try in vain to deliver a lot more than what students are capable of grasping, in the hope that I can take them to the next level. But staying grounded along with them tends to be a lot more rewarding for both myself and my students.

Great speakers also tend to have a general theme around which their speech revolves (like Subroto Bagchi's on managing change). This helps the listeners stay focused. While they may take slight detours to focus on some parallel areas, they keep coming back to their central theme. Contrast this with speakers who talk about a number of things and then summarize. I see these speeches as having different modules that are independent of each other. One definite advantage of this approach is that the listener is never lost and can pick up from anywhere in the middle of the speech because of their independent nature. But the drawback is that the impact of the speech on the listener is reduced. The takeaways will mostly be a few, if any, among the list of things the speaker spoke about.

I have been lucky to have been taught and guided by some great teachers. I have realized that while some among them might have been natural speakers, their greatness came from their preparedness. As Ranjana Kumar puts it, luck is when preparedness meets opportunity.

Reflections on career advice

When graduating, while there is a sense of relief from a burden, deep within, we all know that it is only being replaced with a bigger burden. We now need to be more responsible, worthy of a degree that was conferred upon us, apply what we learnt, guide society and lead a few others who did not get the opportunity that we did. Commencement speeches come at the right time to congratulate us on the success we are celebrating, and also to guide us through our fleeting and sometimes scary thoughts on our responsibility.

Tasks always look daunting in the beginning. But as the saying goes, 'a task well begun is half done'. Ajay Banga refers to this when he talks about our first night at the university. Very often, we are scared to begin. We question our capabilities. But once we start, we realize that we are well capable of going with the flow. So, if the convocation marks a new beginning, how can we make the beginning?

The first approach may be to sustain our willingness to learn more. While we think the convocation marks the end of our learning, the speeches are gentle reminders that it only marks a newer phase in our learning. We need to be constantly aware of the fact that our knowledge will soon become obsolete, as change is the only thing permanent. Deepak Parekh also mentions that making mistakes and accepting our ignorance is the first step. Indra Nooyi hints at the same, imploring us to be curious and read voraciously. At educational institutions, the most important thing we learn is to learn. The PhD programme taught me humility, among other things. We should remember not to forget this basic lesson. Learning to train our intuition and to be creative is tough, but they are skills we must learn.

One sign that we are learning is the mistakes we commit as we go. This aspect was focused on by most speakers when they talked about our fear of making mistakes. It was comforting to hear that blunders were OK, but more importantly, the speakers encouraged us to make mistakes. This is based on the presumption that our mistakes occur despite careful planning, and are evidence that we try new things and innovate. Hence, we need the courage to take risks, for the greatest return may lie where the greatest risk is. And as Gopalakrishnan points out, some mistakes can be avoided if we are aware of contextual knowledge and our tendency to overestimate our solutions.

As we learn and progress, we are given more power. In fact, a degree also makes many of us 'powerful'. We might next own a company or a division, a team and whatnot. While this could bring fear to some, it also brings a sort of arrogance. The arrogance reduces our ability to reflect and make appropriate decisions. But the speakers suggest a way out and ask us to remember our primary roles. When Arun Maira stresses that leaders are trustees, not owners, we realize our actual role. This humility will help us discharge our duties in a more appropriate and efficient manner. Banga also summarizes that a leader should have a sense of the urgency and balance in any situation.

Like power, we need to understand the role of money in our life, because if we assume money to be powerful, we risk engaging in a perennial chase after wealth. As we begin our careers, some of us have pretty hefty starting packages, and some of us lighter. Especially when there is daylight between an industrial salary and academic salary, one does wonder if we made the right career choice. Of course, we enjoy the freedom and, more than that, the satisfaction that comes from doing our job. And when we hear Aroon Purie saying that what matters is the passion with which we do the job, however simple the job is, we feel vindicated. Parekh implored us not to chase money and says that the passion with which we do our job will automatically bring forth wealth.

More importantly, almost all the speakers stressed on both passion and compassion. Banga considers this as 'doing well and doing good'. There are many who are passionate, but there are only a few who are compassionate as well. We must not only focus on the size of the purse but also on the size of the purpose (R. Mukundan). Arundhati includes this in one of her three Cs.

One of my concerns in teaching was the repetitiveness that comes from teaching the same course over and over again. Though I understand that improvements can always be made, and that there is an added necessity of being current, I was not totally convinced. So when I read Roopa Kudva's experience on how excellence comes from repetition, it was reassuring. And when she says that getting bored is an enemy of excellence, it was more than a gentle nudge in the right direction.

Another great takeaway from our education process is the network of friends we get acquainted with. The like-mindedness only increases with the advanced level of the degree. While it is important to be in touch and sustain some of these relationships, it is equally important to develop this network. Wherever we go, forming friendships and building the network can be crucial to our contribution. The 'Sat Sang', as it is referred to, not only supports our endeavours, but also gives us multiple perspectives and could also act as a check to our adverse reactions.

Most of us grow up in an atmosphere where comparison with others was inevitable. This is not only inefficient, but many a time detrimental to our progress. It is important for us to get away from this mentality. Yes, it is good to show some urgency as Banga said, but the reason for that urgency should be us lagging behind our own excellence benchmarks. While competition should drive us, it should not consume us. There is great joy in enjoying spontaneity in life and relishing the little things. Internal satisfaction and harmonizing our self

(Ravichandran) will not only release us from the burden of stress, it will makes us channel our energy to our true purpose.

Almost all the speakers stressed on the importance of being steadfast when it comes to ethics and integrity. Examples galore for traps that people have fallen into and how shortcuts have led to failure eventually, if not immediately. At the same time, we may also have moments when, for no fault of ours, injustice is meted out to us. It is at these times that we need to channel our anger to productive means as Gopalakrishnan suggests.

I used to think my time at IIT Madras would be my golden days. Then came the experience at the University of Rochester. I will no doubt cherish the good times I had at both these places. But when Anand Mahindra warns us that the greatest danger for us is if we let these memories remain our best, it sends us a reminder. True, they were great memories. But we must vow to create memories that will be even better.

Maira describes three scenarios for our country. Muddling along, falling apart and the flotilla advancing. To a certain extent, it reflects the way our careers may progress. The conflict in our case is between our true purpose, short-term goals and the way we function. If our compass is not aligned with the rest of our self, we will either be muddling along or falling apart.

Thanks to the Internet, a few years ago, I got access to Steve Jobs's commencement speech at Stanford. The words 'Stay hungry, stay foolish' will remain forever in my memory. Many of the convocation speeches I read in this collection belong to the same class. They make you pause and think, no matter what stage of your career you are currently on. Above all, we must constantly ponder on our true purpose. To quote A.P.J. Abdul Kalam, 'enquiring and committed minds with a mission focus produced dramatic results—what is yours?'

Acknowledgements

It is a pleasure to acknowledge the contributors and speakers who helped me put this volume together.

Mr S. Santhanam, a retired employee of the Indian Institute of Management Ahmedabad, and a good friend, managed the initial correspondences.

Dr Sundaravalli Narayanaswami, a colleague in IIM Ahmedabad, provided the technical support in putting the document together.

Thanks to the speakers and the authors for their permission to include their work in this compilation.

To Radhika and her team at Penguin Random House for their support in transforming the compilation from a manuscript to a book.

To a friend who would like to remain anonymous for giving final touches to the compilation.